To Kenny

with best love

Mum + Dad.

Xmas 1961

MODERN TROUT FISHING

WAITING FOR THE RISE—page 75

MODERN TROUT FISHING

BY

W. CARTER PLATTS

WITH SIXTEEN PLATES
AND NINETEEN LINE ILLUSTRATIONS

LONDON
ADAM & CHARLES BLACK

FIRST PUBLISHED 1938
REPRINTED 1942
SECOND EDITION 1947
THIRD EDITION 1954
FOURTH EDITION 1961

A. AND C. BLACK LTD
4, 5 AND 6 SOHO SQUARE, LONDON, W.I

MADE IN GREAT BRITAIN
PRINTED BY R. & R. CLARK, LIMITED, EDINBURGH

PREFACE

THIS volume is the result of an honest effort to describe, with such impartiality as I am capable of, the many and various legal methods of catching trout with rod and line in common usage to-day in the British Isles.

Probably over no branch of angling has controversy raged more furiously than over trout fishing, but propaganda has no intentional part in these pages, which, I trust, will be found free from hysterical partisanship. If, however, any apology is called for, then, "with 'bated breath and whispering humbleness", I crave forgiveness of the fly fisher for having devoted so much space to bait fishing, while, with equal humility, I entreat the pardon of the bait fisher for allotting so many pages to fly fishing.

Except incidentally, I have not dealt with fly-fishers' entomology, and what references I have made to that fascinating study are of necessity very brief. Should the reader be desirous of extending his knowledge of the natural insects his flies imitate—or are supposed to imitate—he is recommended to consult W. G. Bainbridge's *The Fly-fisher's Guide to Aquatic Flies* (A. & C. Black, Ltd. 5s.).

To the proprietors of *The Field* and *The Salmon and Trout Magazine* I am indebted for permission to include matter from articles of mine which have appeared in their publications, and to my friends, H. D. Turing and G. E. M. Skues, I offer grateful thanks for the assistance they have given me in preparing the following pages.

Dr E. A. Barton, prince of South Country angling photographers, has laid me under a deep debt of gratitude by furnishing the two charming illustrations of chalk stream angling, "Will the Trout take it?" and "Waiting for the Rise". The two fine pictures, "Typical Wet-fly Water on the Ribble" and "Reservoir Fishing", are inserted by courtesy of *The Yorkshire Post*. The Irish Tourist Association very kindly contribute the photographs, "May-fly Dapping on Lough Corrib" and "Sea Trout Fishing in Connemara", the Canadian Pacific Railway that of "Trout Fishing in Canada", and P. D. Malloch that of "A Good Dish from Loch Leven".

W. C. P.

1938.

CONTENTS

vii

ILLUSTRATIONS

PRINTED SEPARATELY FROM THE TEXT

PRINTED IN THE TEXT

MODERN TROUT FISHING

CHAPTER I

TROUT AND TROUT FISHING

Oh, they're landin' *Salmo fario*; you can hear the music play—
The music of the merry reel when troutie darts away.
The boys are at the river, where they've been since peep o' day,
  Their downy beds an' breakfustesses scornin'.

They are landing *Salmo fario*; they 'ave caught 'im on the rise;
They're a-ticklin' of 'is appetite wi' artificial flies.
'Is greed'll be 'is ruin, an' we'll soon see 'ow 'e fries—!
  Oh, they're landin' *Salmo fario* in the mornin'!

IN Scotland the salmon may be eulogised by its special
band of devotees as Lord of the Loch and Monarch of
the Stream, and I have no word but of praise to say of
the glorious thrills engendered by the gallant fight it
puts up in its struggle for freedom from the "envenomed
stang that thro' its lugs gies many a twang" when the
iron enters its jaw, if not its soul.

But, ranged alongside the hordes of trout fishers, the
salmon anglers on our British waters—especially our
English waters—are few in number, and even the late
P. D. Malloch, Scottish salmon angler as he was, and
saturated with salmon lore, unequivocally asserts, in his
Salmon, Sea Trout, and other Freshwater Fish, that "to the
angler the common yellow trout is by far the most
important fish that swims, for more people capture
it than any other living thing. The pleasure derived
from its capture, too, surpasses that of any other sport,

1

while interest in the study of the trout seems to be inexhaustible."

Nor can our love of the trout and trout fishing be regarded as the insular prejudice of a conservative people, for a famous American angler, Dr Charles F. Holder, after a visit to our shores, wrote, in his *Game Fishes of the World*, "I can imagine no purer delight than to wander along these beautiful streams of England, casting here and there with the daintiest of tackle, dropping a dry fly into the circle of radiations formed by the rising trout".

So far as I may judge, angling possesses a greater wealth of literature than any other outdoor sport, and it is significant of the high regard in which we hold trout fishing that that branch of the gentle craft is the predominating feature in our angling library. A glance along my own angling bookshelves, which are fairly representative, leads me to opine that as much space in angling literature is devoted to trout fishing as to all the other branches of the sport combined.

There is a fascinating glamour about trout and trout fishing unshared by any other British fish. It is a sort of national institution, to which, once under its spell, even the exiled Briton in the uttermost parts of the earth is ever the willing slave. It follows the flag. It has been said that in settling a colony the English pioneer first relieves the natives of their fears, then relieves them of their land, after which he builds a church and rolls out a cricket crease. It only remains to be added that, this done, he sends home for a consignment of trout ova, with which to stock the streams, and the colony is then considered to be established on a firm and lasting foundation. Throughout the Dominions excellent trout fishing, the consequence of the importation of British trout, is available to the colonist.

At home, trout fishing was never more popular than it is to-day, and never were there so many trout fishers. Improved transport facilities have brought once inaccessible waters, figuratively, to the doors of the town dwellers, and the big amalgamations have rented trout lengths which have added to the contemplative delights of float fishing for coarse fish the higher joys of trout fishing at a charge to the angler that is almost infinitesimal. I have before me particulars of the stocking of such a preserve with 1900 two-year-olds at a cost of £95.[1] And the charge to members of the clubs in the amalgamation for fishing this trout preserve is 6d. per day!

Compare this exceedingly modest fee with the charges on a seven-miles length of a famous South Country chalk stream: £200 per annum, 75 guineas per month, 20 guineas per week, 4 guineas per day. These are extreme cases, and there is a vast difference in the nature of the sport with which they are concerned. Still, throughout the provinces it is, speaking generally, not difficult to enjoy the privileges afforded by angling clubs of limited membership on really high-class water for an annual subscription of five guineas or thereabout, while season, or short date, tickets for fairly decent trout fishing are obtainable at much lower rates. Here and there, in out-of-the-way districts, one may fish freely on sufferance of the agricultural occupiers, and, even where main streams are preserved privately or by clubs, enjoyable sport is often to be had on tributary brooks and becks.

Moreover, the name is legion of the country hotels providing trout fishing facilities for their guests either free or at a moderate charge, while the rule seems to be that the further north the angler travels, the more easily does he find access to good trout fishing. Thus the

---

[1] The present cost of this number of fish might be anything between £200 and £800, according to their size, but the comparison quoted remains valid in principle.

3

country offers trout fishing to suit every purse, and, more, to chime with the varying tastes of its votary.

Does he love to loiter, in sweet expectation of the rise, beside some gently flowing flood that lies

> Deep-meadow'd, happy, fair with orchard lawns
> And bowery hollows,

wherein fat golden-sided rascals lurk, ready to match their critical discernment against the deftly dressed and paraffinointed dun, daintily riding the smiling ripples? Then the South Country chalk stream, that winds through the water-meadows and tangled boscage from hatch-hole to hatch-hole, will minister to his cravings, while "a swete ayre of the swete fauours of the meede floures makyth hym hungry, and he hereth the melodyous armony of fowles ".

Or, maybe, his thoughts turn longingly to the broad rolling river, where, thigh-deep in mid-current, he may "chuck it" while the trout "chance it". The wider moorland rivers of the West and North Country, brawling and babbling to the wild whaup of the curlew and the plaintive cry of the wheeling peewit, what time his leash of hackled flies combs the hastening waves for the lively knock-abouts seeking what they may devour, will fill his soul with content and his basket with trout "while yet the dark-brown water aids the guile".

To put it in a nutshell, trout fishing, if not a panacea for all ills, is a kind of cornucopia for the gratification of all angling fancies, including those of the fly fisher (wet or dry), the minnow spinner, the float fisher, the bottom fisher, the dibber, the troller, the May-fly dapper, the nocturnal "bustard" fisher—in short, from that of the humblest disciple, whose preparation consists largely of grubbing up a worm with his heel, to him of the advanced scientific school, who hatches the

Trout Fishing in Canada

FISHING THE MOORLAND RIVER—page 11

daintiest artificial flies out of silk and feathers under Sam Weller's "double million magnifying gas microscope of hextra power". Trout fishing is at once the purist's dream and the pot-hunter's delight. It offers health to the valetudinarian, food to the hungry, solace to the oppressed, and—it is even maliciously suggested —stimulation to the imaginative.

To delve into the ichthyological problems that surround the trout would be outside the scope of this book, yet it may be permissible to add here a brief note or two which may interest the trout fisher.

A generation ago it was popularly supposed that there were many distinct species of trout swimming our British waters, such as the Brown Trout (*Salmo fario*), Sea Trout (*Salmo trutta*), Great Lake Trout (*Salmo ferox*), Gillaroo Trout (*Salmo stomachicus*), Loch Leven Trout (*Salmo levenensis*), and Slob Trout (*Salmo estuarius*). Modern research, however, has convinced our scientists that all the above, and several more, are but variations, brought about by environment or hereditary habit, of one common species, the *Salmo trutta* of Linnæus. At the same time it will be long before the old title of *Salmo fario* is ousted from everyday parlance as the convenient means of indicating the English brown or brook trout.

And to what size may the trout fisher expect his catch, individually, to run? If he is ambitious to beat the British record he will have to land something in the near vicinity of 40 lb., for the present record is claimed for a trout of 39½ lb. caught on Loch Awe in 1866.[1] Another of 30½ lb. is held to have been caught on Lough Derg in 1861, while, if we include Dominion waters, a 30-pounder was taken on Lake Rotorua, New Zealand, in 1923. A slob trout was landed on Loch Stennis, in

[1] This fish is not recognised as the record trout by the British Record (Rod-caught) Fish Committee.

1

Orkney, in 1889 which weighed 29 lb., but it was caught on a set line, not with a rod. The late Duke of Rutland, in his Trout volume of the "Fur, Feather and Fin Series", mentions a trout of 27½ lb. caught on the Tay with fly as the largest river trout, and this is closely followed by one of 27¼ lb., landed on the Inver in 1870.

But these are historic events, not everyday occurrences, and the average weight of the fish the trout fisher may reasonably expect to encounter varies to a very wide extent according to the character of the water he is fishing. Thus, on the tiny upland burns and streamlets of the North and West the great majority of the troutlets may not go beyond a couple of ounces. On the moorland rivers 4-oz. fish may be looked for, with an occasional half-pounder as a special prize ; though on the same rivers, on favoured lengths where the feed is abundant, the trout may average three to the pound, and three-quarter-pounders, and even pounders, may find their way into the creel. Little can be said of what may be expected on the lakes. One loch may be crowded—overcrowded—with small fish, while a neighbouring loch may yield trout fewer in number but of noble proportions. In Loch Leven the fish average well on to a pound. It is on the chalk streams that the biggest average weight may be looked for, and where two- and three-pounders are not uncommon, having waxed fat largely on the abundance of food bred in the weed beds.

It is difficult to estimate with any exactness the natural length of life of the average trout. Scale reading, useful as it is in many respects, is apt to be misleading in making such a calculation, seeing that the vast majority of the scales read are those of fish which have had their natural span cut short by fatal accidents with hooks in them. Still, I think we may safely opine that, escaping the perils that beset its course through life, the trout may enjoy a round dozen of years of existence before it succumbs to senile decay.

Of these twelve years they are free risers up to, say, the completion of the fourth year. They then gradually become less keen on a surface diet, and, in inverse ratio, develop their bottom-feeding and cannibalistic instincts. For the remainder of their allotted spell, say the last four or five years, they are positive pests in the fishery ; they are almost entirely cannibal, of no use to the fly fisher, and the bait fisher has the satisfaction of knowing that every time he captures one he is benefiting the fishery.

The trout usually attains a takeable size during its third year, which is expressed by the pisciculturist's formula of 2 +.

Finally to this introductory chapter, here are some lines I came across in A. Nelson Bromley's *A Fly Fisher's Reflections*, which seem to carry the spirit of old Dickie Routledge's advice, when, somebody having asked him what was the most killing fly on the Eden, replied, "The flee that's always in the watter":

> Chance governs all: keep casting still
> Nor ever let kind hope forsake you;
> Just where you least expect he will,
> A fish may take you.

CHAPTER II

TROUT RODS

In his novitiate the trout fisher commences his search for the ideal rod that, banishing all suggestion of weariness to the flesh, will make the mere act of casting a dream of pure delight and induce a constant procession of fish from the pool to the pannier. By and by comes disillusionment, as the lurking suspicion is born within him that it is the man behind the rod that matters most, and, in his pessimistic moments, he is forced to the conclusion that, within liberal limits, the born fly fisher can cast with anything, and the born duffer can cast with nothing.

There is at least a modicum of truth in the first clause of the dictum. One of the most successful fly fishers I ever knew could do wonders in the way of casting with the most ill-adapted tools. At one time he fished with a bean-pole—at any rate it felt like a bean-pole when I handled it—and made exquisite casts. After the huge and ugly bean-pole he picked up a delicate little greenheart from a tackle-dealer's "selling off" list, and this was followed by an atrociously stiff whole-cane that was strengthened and sustained and braced and crossgartered like a comic opera bandit with a steel lattice; yet, to the observer, these vagarious changes made no appreciable difference to the grace and effectiveness of his casts.

At the same time, there is not the slightest doubt that, while the versatile angler may, in case of need, adapt

8

himself, with more or less success, to the idiosyncrasies of the casually acquired rod, he will fish with far more comfort and far less fatigue with the weapon whose balance and action are suited to his physique and style.

In the days of grandfatherdom various woods were largely employed in the manufacture of trout rods, particularly ash, hickory, lancewood and greenheart, in addition to whole-cane and split-cane to a limited extent. To-day the woods, with the exception of greenheart, have disappeared from the rod-maker's repertory, and his attention is mostly confined to that timber, split-cane, and whole-cane.

Within living memory—if one is well in the running for octogenarian honours—the modern trout rod has undergone many processes of evolution from the cumbersome weapon of the mid-Victorian age to the dainty, yet powerful, tool of to-day. Thanks to the improvements effected, we now *fish* for trout where our grandfathers *flailed* with prodigiously long, double-handed implements.

Gradually rods were shortened, the single-handed pattern came into vogue and, for the angler unaccustomed to live laborious days, filled a long-felt want. Especially for fly rods greenheart found its way into the front rank of public favour—deservedly so—and was, and is, greatly esteemed for its steel-like properties. It is the most useful timber that has been pressed into the rod-making service; but, unfortunately, it has an occasional tendency to snap precisely at the critical moment when it "didn't orter". I have a strong suspicion, founded on actual fact in a few instances, that a large proportion of these breakages are due to the fact that the strips from which the pieces are fashioned are *sawn* from the plank, in which case the grain of the wood is apt to run diagonally across the rod instead of longitudinally. If the strips are riven from the plank the grain runs straight up and down the rod and retains its full power of resistance. I call to mind one greenheart top of mine which broke along the grain, and that grain ran out at one side of the rod less than six inches below the spot at which it entered at the other side.

Gradually, too, the split-cane rod, built up of six longitudinal sections of bamboo, emerged from what might be regarded as its experimental stage into the region of popular utility, and up to now has remained the first choice of the majority of rod connoisseurs. But steel possesses qualities so peculiarly desirable in fly rods that rod-makers long ago commenced to toy with the idea of incorporating its strength and elasticity in cane rods. Thus we came to have the steel-centred split-canes, in which a steel core—practically a steel wire—is built in the centre of the weapon. Controversy has raged fiercely over the advantages claimed for this combination, the adverse critics maintaining that the presence of the steel core sets up internal friction and disintegration in the heart of the rod. Anyhow, the well-made split-cane trout rod needs no steel centre; it is quite efficient without it.

During the last few years a movement has been afoot to introduce the tubular steel rod to the British angler. It has already established itself in America, and, after handling both fly and bait-casting rods of this type, I am convinced that the steel trout rod is the rod of the future. The supercilious angler's sneer that he preferred to do his trout fishing otherwise than with nine feet of gas-pipe is as vacuous as were the jeers with which the unbeliever greeted the introduction of steel shafts for golf clubs, now popular all the world over.

It is true that attempts have been made to find a market in this country for cheap imported American steel rods, but without any conspicuous success. One angling friend of mine bought half a dozen of them on the chance that he might find a good one among the lot. He didn't. Now, however, British makers of a world-famed steel golf shaft are turning out tubular steel rods which are as superior to the cheap Yankee stuff as our best English-made split-canes are superior to the cheap, trashy imported ones. Finished in the highest style with cork handles, agate rings where desirable, stainless steel ferrules, and beautifully enamelled, they combine power with delicacy and perfect action. Their weight is no more than that of the best split-canes and their price is a little lower. (*See note on page* 15.)

On the rival merits of the split-cane and the greenheart rods opinions differ, though the majority of anglers prefer the former. The greenheart is cheaper; it is also heavier. The split-cane is more powerful and will stand more rough usage. I have one 10½-ft. split-cane that was made for me forty years ago. It has fished wet fly and dry fly, clear-water worm and minnow, and has also had its share of swimming the worm for winter grayling; and it is, apparently, as capable as ever it was.

Now, though I plead guilty to having indulged myself in a multiplicity of trout rods, I quite realise that the man, fishing the moorland river subject to sudden vicissitudes of condition, who sticks to one general utility rod saves himself a lot of worry. Take the case of the other trout fisher with a rack full of rods and a day's opportunity to use them. Which is he to take? Will yesterday's rain bring down a heavy turbid tide, and call for the use of his special worm rod? Or will the waxing waters merely reach a bold minnow height, in which circumstances he will not be happy unless he has his special minnow rod? Or, again, will the land, the thirsty land, have absorbed the main of yesterday's downfall except the two or three inches necessary to produce an ideal fly water? In this case, of course, no peace of mind would be possible without the company of his 6-oz. split-cane fly rod.

And so he wastes valuable fishing time and courts needless brain fag by worrying over the problem of which rod to take, when he knows full well—or ought to know—that whichever he selects is bound to be the wrong one, while all the time his humbler neighbour, who cheerfully carries on with the same old rod for fly, minnow, and worm, has been slogging away at the river for hours, getting the cream of the sport no matter what state the river happened to be in.

Even if the question of bait fishing be excluded, it is a good plan to have a fly rod that will serve for both wet and dry work. Formerly it was the general opinion that a special rod was a necessity in fishing the dry fly, an opinion which arose, no doubt, from the fact that many of the fly rods of that day were too whippy to drive a heavy line into the wind. And some of them *were* whippy, embodying what was known as the "Castle Connell" action, playing right down to the hand in an unmistakable fashion. Long years ago the fancy took me to possess myself of one of these "Castle Connell" wobblers. It was a single-handed 13-footer that tapered both ways, but, of course, more towards the top. Still, it was actually a little thicker in the middle than where it entered the grip.

Having been nurtured in the faith that a fly rod should be stiffish in the butt, and gradually increase in pliancy towards the top, my first efforts with my new possession created in me a strong impression of the probable behaviour of a weak-kneed, inverted pendulum in an advanced state of intoxication. However, as I got to know it better—and as it got to know me—we worried

" —— AND LANDING "

Typical Wet-fly Water on the Ribble—page 61

along very comfortably together. It required a considerable effort to start the thing off at the commencement of a cast, but once you had supplied the initial impetus, and acquired the guiding knack, and overcome that sinking feeling that the rod was about to snap like a carrot immediately above your hand, it went through its little performance almost automatically, and delivered the goods at the correct address. I did not use it for fly fishing; it was far too slow in the strike; but for some years, although at first sight it might appear a very unsuitable weapon for the purpose, I fished clear-water worm and clear-water minnow (before the advent of the light-casting spool reel) with it with great content to myself and a certain amount of discomfort to the trout.

Nowadays trout fly rods of split-cane, greenheart or steel are to be had, with enough backbone to stand the drive and false-casting of dry-fly work, and yet delicate enough to lay a leash of wet flies on the stream as gently as a mother's caress. Indeed, rod-makers now produce rods specially designed for the dual purpose of dry-fly and wet-fly fishing.

For such a rod, although for dry fly alone a shorter weapon finds favour with many anglers, 10 ft. or $10\frac{1}{2}$ ft. will be found a suitable length. The next thing to be considered is the balance. This is of far more importance to the comfort of the user than the actual weight of the rod. An ill-balanced 6-oz. rod will tire him much sooner than a well-balanced one of two or three ounces heavier. Equipped with its reel, and the line on the reel, the rod should balance at a point three or four inches above the grip. Should the rod be somewhat top-heavy, but otherwise commendable, the balance can be corrected by introducing a lead washer of suitable thickness between the butt and the rubber button.

Some idea of the whippiness of the rod may be formed by gently waggling it about, and it is often recommended that, to test the quickness of its strike, it should be held horizontally a foot or so above a smooth surface, *e.g.* a table. The strike is then made with a sharp upward turn of the wrist, and the point of the rod flops down and hits the table. From this it is argued that in fishing the upward strike will slacken the line to the extent of the flop before the rod returns to its horizontal position and tightens on the fish. This argument is not altogether sound, as, in actual fishing, the weight of some yards of heavy line, in dry-fly work, is dependent from the point of the rod and acts as a curb. The weight of a wet line, with the pull of the water as well, may impose still greater restraint; it is only when the rod top is free from encumbrance that it flops really badly. However, the flop of the free top teaches something. If it flops very little, the action is probably too stiff; if it flops badly—and especially if it is slow in springing back—the chances are that it will fail to hook many fish.

Until the last few years no high-class rod was considered "it" unless it were fitted with lock-fast joints. These did their work well in preventing many throwouts. The timorous may still prefer them, but plain suction ferrules are now made with such microscopic exactness of fit that no additional precaution is necessary.

It is advisable to have agate rings for the one nearest the butt and the one at the top. The intermediate rings may be of the snake pattern; there are none better.

After use the rod should be wiped dry, and, whether kept in a case or not, the pieces should lie or hang straight. It has long been my practice to hang all my rods, each piece separate, by its topmost ring from a hook on a rack. Each piece then hangs perfectly straight down and does not acquire a bias. The inner ferrules should be smeared lightly with vaseline.

Other rods for special purposes will be described in later chapters dealing with the styles of angling for which they are respectively suitable.

NOTE

There are now fibre-glass rods as well as steel rods, and both types are marketed by British firms. The best makers have tried to bring the performance of rods made in the new materials as near as possible to that of the natural materials, and not merely to undercut the price. Would-be purchasers need, therefore, expect no prejudice against them. The difference now is largely that between an engineering product and a piece of craftsmanship. Particular ranges of fly and spinning rods in the two mediums have reached a high standard of mechanical perfection. The fisherman must decide for himself whether the subtle qualities which craft can impart to split-cane and greenheart are also obtainable in fibre-glass or steel.

CHAPTER III

OTHER TACKLE

THE first essential to the perfect combination of rod and reel is that, in the manner described in the last chapter, the latter should balance the former. As the philosopher remarked, "What is the good of a tenpenny nail if you've only a ha'penny hammer?" Beyond that, what is asked of the reel is that it should hold thirty yards of dressed fly line and about the same length of finer backing; it should be narrow in the drum to enable a quick recovery of line; and it should be furnished with an optional check sufficiently powerful to put a reasonable amount of restraint on the headlong rush of a fish, but not strong enough to invite a breakage. The backing plays a dual rôle; it gives the angler extra length when the occasional sockdologer is encountered, and it pads the inner part of the drum, so that the most used part of the line lies in larger coils upon it and can, consequently, be more speedily reeled up. In some reels the check is adjustable by means of a screw to the minutest gradations of power.

The fly-fishing reel may be $3\frac{1}{4}$ inches to $3\frac{1}{2}$ inches in diameter, and should be furnished with a line guard consisting of bars across the cage or a large agate ring. This is a precaution against the line fouling itself on the reel. Other details may be left to be determined by the depth of the purchaser's pocket. The fixed-spool and other spinning reels will be dealt with in the chapter on spinning.

16

The fly line next claims attention. This should be of dressed plaited silk of the double tapered variety, *i.e.* while the bulk of the line is level in thickness, the last four or five yards at each end taper off to a fine point. To this fine point is attached the thick end of the tapered cast, which, itself, fines down to 3X or 4X gut, and so a continuous taper through line and cast is assured, and this much facilitates casting and lays the cast straight on the water instead of, more or less, "all of a heap". The advantage of the double taper is that, as the reel line becomes shorter through the necessity of cutting away worn portions at its junction with the cast, it can be reversed and the other tapered end brought into service. Even then, of course, the level portion of the line remains in good fettle after both ends are worn out; but it need not be scrapped, as short-end tapers are now obtainable, and can be spliced on the line to replace the worn-out parts. They can also be used for converting a level line into a tapered one.

The waterproofing of the line is a long and laborious job. It may occupy six months, and consists mainly of repeatedly soaking (in some instances under the air-pump) in raw linseed oil, drying, rubbing down and polishing, and is little likely to be undertaken by the amateur. An easy method, but not lasting, is to soak the line by running it through melted paraffin wax, squeezing off the surplus dope as it emerges, and rubbing well with some such approved dressing as Cerolene or Ceroleum. This dressing is good as long as it lasts, but requires repeating at intervals of a few months. When I have had occasion to use this method I have melted the wax on the hob in an earthen jam jar until it was in a thin liquid state. Then, having procured an iron nut, I have threaded the line through it, dropped the nut into the melted liquid—which I have kept in a thin state by standing it on a hot iron plate after removal from the hob—and drawn the line through, running it between finger and thumb as it has emerged so that the surplus wax has fallen into the jar.

Much faulty casting, as well as unnecessary fatigue, is caused by the use of too light a line. The line should be heavy enough to give the rod something to do without overtaxing it. When line and rod are well matched, the latter, by its resilience, will do a good share of the work. The surface of the waterproofed line should be quite smooth, but should not have a high glossy finish. If it has it is liable to crack, let in the water, and rapidly deteriorate.

After use the line should be run off the reel either on to a line-drier or coiled lightly on a newspaper until it is perfectly dry. Once it gets "tacky" the fault may be temporarily remedied by various specifics recommended for the job; but it is very rare that it can be permanently remedied. A good line, well treated, will last for several years, and such a line as I have indicated will serve for fishing dry fly, wet fly, upstream worm, and Creeper and Stone-fly.

Any undressed fine and strong line, silk or flax, will serve for backing, but I prefer it treated with paraffin wax in the manner I have described. It preserves it from rot.

We come now to the cast. Before the general adoption of silk-worm gut for making up casting lines, horsehair was commonly used for that purpose, and on the moorland rivers, where the trout do not average more than half a pound, there are many old anglers who still use it and, when they can get it, will have no other. It has advantages over gut. It is more elastic; it does not fray; it delivers the flies more lightly; droppers tied on it do not lovingly entwine themselves round the cast; it does not rot like gut; and entanglements with hair are far more rare than with gut. One North Country veteran once confessed to me, "If ever I steal a horse it will be for its tail".

The hair should be round and sound, and the most highly prized is that from the tail of a white stallion. It is translucent, and has not the objectional glitter of gut.

Practically all the angler's gut comes from Spain, and is the product of the silkworm. Each worm possesses two glands containing a sticky fluid which, in the natural order of things, would be exuded in the form of the silken thread forming the cocoon. But in gut manufacture, when the worm is on the point of commencing to spin, it is thrown into a vinegar bath, and the two glands, which harden into threads on exposure to the air, are extracted by the nimble fingers of the workers, drawn to their full length, and dried. This is the raw gut. It goes through many processes before it reaches the angler, graded into its varying thicknesses. However, the natural gut, which we know as undrawn, is still much too thick for the finer branches of angling, and to fit it for these it is drawn through holes in metal plates, which scrape off the outer covering, and reduce it to 1X, 2X, 3X, 4X, or even 6X and 7X. It is then known as drawn gut, and, I am sorry to say, there seems to be no universal standard operative in grading these finer counts, one firm's 6X being no finer than another firm's 4X for instance. In diminishing scale undrawn gut of interest to the trout fisher is graded as Regular, Fina, and Refina, the latter being the finest undrawn.

In recent years the use of silkworm gut has been supplanted to some, and an increasing, extent by a manufactured article popularly known as Japanese gut, or gut substitute, which is marketed under various trade names. It possesses characteristics which would entitle it to claim kinship with the little girl who had a little curl right down the middle of her forehead, for "when it is good it is very, very good, and when it is bad it is horrid".

In the preparation of this artificial gut, the basis of which is silk, the worm is allowed to complete its cocoon, when the silk is worked into a thread of the desired thickness, and this is passed through a boiling mixture of animal glue and an extract of seaweed. The silk is thus not only saturated with the dope, but might almost be said to become amalgamated with it. It is then dried with the aid of chemicals, and polished. *(See note on page 28.)*

Obviously the process lends itself to the practice of "ways that are dark and tricks that are vain" in the hands of the unscrupulous. Cotton may be mixed with the silk, or too much glue-cum-seaweed dope and too little silk may be used, in the effort to cheapen the product. It is understood that in the best gut substitute 85 per cent of pure silk should be incorporated, and to ensure getting a good article the angler should buy only the well-known brands of the leading tackle-dealers.

Thickness for thickness gut substitute is stronger than gut, but it does not last so long. Its great advantage is that it is obtainable in any length up to 100 yards, which obviates the necessity of knotting short lengths together, as is the case with gut. Indeed, this absence of knots permits it to be used, in its finer grades, as a reel line in spinning. Another recommendation is its comparative cheapness.

Both gut and gut substitute are brittle when dry. Consequently it is necessary to soak them before knotting them or fishing with them, and the substitute requires much longer soak than the gut. Half an hour may suffice to soak gut; hours may vanish into the *ewigkeit* before the substitute is rendered thoroughly pliable. It is not a bad plan to place the substitute in tepid water—some say a 50-50 mixture of water and glycerine—and let it soak overnight.

Formerly the notion was current that the staining of gut light blue rendered it less visible to the trout, as the blue in the cast merged with the blue in the sky against which the fish viewed it. This theory overlooked the fact that an opaque body seen against the light is always dark whatever its colour. However, later research has taught us something of underwater optics, and has revealed to us the fact that the trout only sees the sky through a small circular "window" above it, and that a submerged line, beyond the area of that "window", is seen against a reflection of the bottom of the stream, the reflection being broken up to some extent by the surface ripples. Consequently the blue tinting of the cast is useless ; rather should it be coloured so that, in optical effect, it merges into the reflection of the bottom—dark if the bottom be of mud, mottled if it be of gravel.

The way in which my thoughts were seriously turned to the colour question in connection with casting-lines was amusing. In a Press article on the use of horsehair for fishing purposes, I had bemoaned the fact that good, long, sound hair was difficult to obtain. In response I received a big bunch of mustangs' hair from the Far West from an unknown friend. It was splendid stuff— long and strong—but, alas! it was dark brown, almost black. "Utterly hopeless!" I murmured, as I laid it mournfully on my study table. It lay there for weeks— except when I took it up to lament over it that it was not white, or even light chestnut.

Now, when I lived in mid-Wharfedale I often fished

with a noted Yorkshire fly fisher, William Brumfitt, of Otley, the same man who dressed the specimen flies for Pritt's *North Country Trout Flies*, and, more, supplied many of the dressings for the same. After I left the district we kept up a desultory correspondence, his letters invariably ending with the pathetic wail: Could I tell him where he could get some good hair? One of his letters came along while the mustang stuff was still on my hands, and I packed it off to him, with a facetious eulogy of its manifold and excellent qualities, never dreaming that he would take me seriously. Imagine, then, my amazement when an old angling friend came over to see me, and casually observed:

"Oh, by the way, I came across old Brumfitt the other day, fishing. He was in high feather, 'Got hold of some champion hair that Carter Platts had sent him! Never seen anything like it before; it was absolutely "it"!' And he wasn't half pulling 'em out with it."

Later, as if to confirm the efficacy of the mustang hair, Farlow's very successfully introduced Hewitt's gut casts, stained with nitrate of silver, and these, I found, were practically the same colour as the mustang hair. I suggested to Alex. Martin, the Glasgow tackle-dealer, that he should make up some hair casts, for moorland rivers, consisting of alternate strands of white and brown hair. This he did, and he ran them for a considerable time as "Skewbald" casts with a flattering amount of success.

There are now on the market "camouflaged" casts, and "rainbow", and other special brands of coloured casts, which have plainly shown that there is no special virtue in the old-fashioned blue tinting.

In the way of landing-nets there is nothing much better than a good make of the V-shaped, collapsible, knuckle-jointed variety. But it is not perfection. I do not like the leather thong across the open end, and the "straight across" end makes it difficult to get the net under a fish in thin, gravel-bottomed water or in an awkward boulder-girt corner. The pear-shaped net I like best, but the other is more convenient for travelling.

For fishing rough-bottomed moorland rivers with rapid currents there is nothing better than an ash-bowed, pear-shaped net with a 5 ft. tough ash shaft terminating in a steel spike and hook like a miniature boat-hook. In wading the shaft acts as a wading staff, the spike securing it from slipping, while the hook is often very useful for pulling down a branch to release your fly when it is hung up in a tree. Also, hooked on to a convenient fence rail or tree branch, it may prove of material assistance in scrambling up a steep bank out of the water.

For use when wading and you require both hands to be at liberty for manipulating your tackle, a very short-handled net will suffice, and quite a serviceable one can be easily made out of a superannuated tennis racket. I have used such a one off and on for years and have found no fault with it.

I wanted to go fishing. The collapsible contraption I had previously used for such fishing as I had in mind was out of order, and the long-shafted arrangement would have been an intolerable nuisance. My eyes fell on a tennis racket that had seen better days, and the rest was easy. Of course, the quickest way would have been simply to have cut away the gut stringing and laced on a net in its place; but there is a lot of unnecessary timber—unnecessary for its improvised purpose—about the handle of a racket. So I took out all the "packing", and retained only the strip of ash that formed the bow and continued down each side of the handle. The two straight ends of the ash strip I screwed

23

and whipped together for the shaft, laced a light net in the bow, and, *voilà!*, my landing-net was complete. Light as the proverbial feather, it can be carried slung on a hook on the creel-strap, or, as I have often carried mine, with the handle simply shoved in the hole of the lid of the creel.

Having caught your trout, in what manner of receptacle are you going to carry them home? Personally I have run the gamut of osier creels, tin creels, wooden creels, and mackintosh bags, but have always reverted to the wicker basket—supplemented with generous-sized pockets, including a "hare" pocket, in my jacket for the portage of the lunch packet, tackle case or fly-book, and other odds and ends. The mackintosh, when not in use, rides well over the lid of the basket if rolled up, and tied with slip-knots, for easy release, to the ends of the creel-strap. The bag lies most snugly to the person, while the wooden creel preserves the fish well. I had one, nicely polished, with a mahogany lid. It was a good creel, but, somehow, when I used it I had an uneasy feeling that the casual observer might harbour a strong suspicion that I had pinched the church voluntary offertory box.

For the conveyance of his fly tackle the wet-fly man will probably choose a fly-book. This should not err on the small size; certainly it should not be less than 6 inches by 4 inches. It should have two leather pockets, accommodation for flies tied on gut and droppers, five or six parchment pockets for gut and casts, and two or three felt leaves for flies on eyed hooks.

The dry-fly man will, no doubt, go in for one of the aluminium fly cases, of which there is such a bewildering variety from which to select that I leave the choice to his fancy, only I would suggest that one fitted with an amadou pad for the drying of water-logged flies saves the trouble of making other provision for carrying that, now, almost essential commodity.

In the way of wading gear, stocking length, *i.e.* just short of the fork, will be found most convenient for trout fishing. To get the most wear out of waders they should be worn alternately right side out and wrong side out. The angler with his waders wrong side out may not look very chic; but that need not trouble him —he is fishing, not doing a Bond Street crawl. Waders wear out first where they have been constantly creased. By adopting the alternative measure the waders are never creased in the same places twice running.

The materials of which wading stockings are made, cotton and rubber, are a very incongruous pair. If you allow the waders to remain damp to keep the rubber nice and cool, you rot the fabric; if you make a point of drying out all the moisure with heat to preserve the fabric, you start up over-vulcanisation of the rubber, which leads it to harden, crack, and leak. Consequently, waders, when not in use, should be kept in a cool but dry place; and immediately after use should be rid of their moisture by being hung, if possible, in a dry draught, but never in heat, whether from the sun's rays or the kitchen range.

Rubber solution for repairing waders you can, of course, buy in tubes. If you want to be assured that you are using only the best, then prepare it yourself. Get— honestly if you can, but get—a piece of pure wild Para rubber. Next to this "plantation smoked sheet" will serve, but Para is the real Mackay. Cut the rubber into shreds—which you easily do if the blade of the knife is kept wet—and place in a jar. Over the rubber pour *mineral* naphtha. Wood naphtha is useless and petrol a poor substitute. Leave the mixture until it has assumed the colour and consistency of treacle. Empty collapsible tubes are to be obtained for a few pence, and can, with the exercise of a little adroitness, be induced to accommodate the sticky concoction.

The space round the leak and the under side of the patch, after being cleaned with a rub of naphtha, should be smeared with the solution, well rubbed in. When they have partially dried to the "tacky" stage, the patch should be applied, pressed well home, and allowed to dry completely under pressure. If the waders are worn habitually right side out the patch should be put on the inside; it is then less liable to be rubbed off.

It is best to wear an additional soft sock *inside* the wader, and, of course, a coarse sock outside between the wader and the brogue.

The question of footwear outside the wading stocking is one of serious importance, as the gripping power of the brogue—or lack of it—may make all the difference between a red-letter day and a coroner's inquest. The rubber sole may be a death-trap, as nothing slips much more readily on a smooth wet surface than rubber. Leather soles should be well studded with hobs. Even then they are usually lacking in holding power at the edge of the soles, and wet leather on smooth submerged stone is slippery. I know. I have tried it. Once I inadvertently trod on a flat, sloping stone with the edge of my brogue, sloshed full length into two feet of water, and the only comfort I got out of the incident was the knowledge that I had been the source of innocent merriment to a couple of casual spectators. Something in the nature of "Alpine" nailing would remedy this weakness.

It is now possible to purchase a brogue which has an outer sole of felt, and a leather heel nailed to the edge, and this is about the nearest approach to the ideal to which we have as yet attained.

Motives of economy may compel one to seek something cheaper than the higher-priced, specially designed brogues. It is a fairly common practice in the North Country to substitute strong laced boots, generously nailed. In such case I earnestly recommend that on no account should boots with three or four pairs of stud hooks at the top be used. One of my angling friends had a narrow escape from drowning through wearing a pair fitted with these hook-on studs, owing to the loop of the lace of one boot catching in one of the studs of the other.

For all-round cheap brogues I do not think the clogs in common use in industrial Lancashire and Yorkshire can be beaten. They are comfortable and do not slip. They are made "Blucher" fashion, with wooden soles armed with irons, heel and sole, that come to the edge of the sole and heel like the horseshoe to the edge of the hoof, thus eliminating the danger I have alluded to.

For summer fishing, however, I have found nothing better than the "rope-soled" canvas boot, the most remarkable thing about which is that it is not better known and appreciated among anglers. It does not slip, and is delightfully light for walking in in hot weather. The only tackle-dealer I know who stocks it is Alex. Martin, of Glasgow.

The handiest way I know of administering the *coup de grâce* to the trout of moorland rivers is by inserting the thumb in the mouth and pressing it against the roof what time the bended forefinger is held against the back of its head, when a sharp turn upward cracks the spine. In dealing with the bigger fish of the chalk streams it is advisable to carry a small priest with which to administer the last rites. For years I have had one consisting of a good sized metal bullet set, drumstick-wise, on the end of a thin five-inch metal rod, the other end of the rod being forked to act, if required, as a disgorger. It is handy and effective.

A pair of small blunt-nosed scissors, which can be carried in the waistcoat pocket, and a knife containing, at least, blade, screw-driver, stiletto, and corkscrew, completes the trout fisher's general equipment.

NOTE

By the perfection of nylon, science has also presented fishermen with alternatives to the traditional materials for lines and casts.

Monofilament nylon, of many different brands, is available in a wide enough range of thicknesses to meet all needs for casts, spinning lines and traces. Their advantages include cheapness, durability, tensile strength, lack of "glitter", and non-absorbency to water which renders soaking unnecessary. A disadvantage is a variation in pliability between one make and another. Some has been found to be too stiff, and some not stiff enough to extend properly when used as a dry-fly cast. Rapid progress in perfecting the new material is eliminating these tendencies. Certain knots, long used with gut and silk, may allow nylon to slip or cause it to break. But safe nylon knots are easy to tie, and a selection is given on page 55.

Still more recent is the introduction of spun nylon and nylon-derivatives as spinning lines or tapered fly lines. At least one make has the dressing "built on" to the line during the manufacturing process. It is claimed that this makes re-dressing unnecessary and tackiness impossible. Again, it is for the individual to decide how the performance of the new lines compares with that of silk lines in casting and floating.

Nylon may be substituted for gut in any of the operations henceforward described for gut. It is, indeed, probably true that it is now used by the majority of fishermen in preference to gut. Its thickness is measured in thousandths of an inch, and the following table shows how these may be interpreted in terms of "x".

Diameter in Inches	x rating	Diameter in Inches	x rating	Diameter in Inches	x rating
0·005	6x	0·011	0/x or 10/5	0·017	4/5
0·006	5x	0·012	9/5	0·018	3/5
0·007	4x	0·013	8/5	0·019	2/5
0·008	3x	0·014	7/5	0·020	1/5
0·009	2x	0·015	6/5	0·021	0/5
0·010	1x	0·016	5/5	0·022	Crown

CHAPTER IV

CASTING THE FLY

THE most artistic and fascinating method of trout fishing is that by which the fish is lured to its doom by the presentation of an artificial fly in a simulated natural manner, and that presentation is known as casting— throwing out the line, with its fly, or flies, attached, so that the feathered morsels fall gently on the water at the desired spot.

There are several more or less orthodox casts to suit the varying circumstances likely to be encountered, and it is when a writer on such matters embarks on the task of describing, adequately and intelligibly, any but the simplest of these he is attempting the impossible. Nor do I hope to succeed where my predecessors and betters have failed. The efforts are frequently accompanied by diagrams of the path of the line or the rod top, which only make confusion worse confounded, for, obviously, it is utterly hopeless to record on a plane surface a series of curves, up and down, to and fro, and sideways. As well might you expect your architect to combine in one drawing the ground plan, front elevation, and side elevation of your new desirable residence.

Nor is the ordinary instantaneous photograph much more enlightening. It may show you the positions of angler and line at the commencement of the cast, at the completion of the first stage, and at the end of the cast; but the varying motions of the line through the air during the intervals is left to the imagination.

To my mind the most effective pictorial representation of casting would be attained by means of a slow-motion film, which should be taken from a point a few yards behind the caster, a few yards to his left, and a few yards above the ground he is standing upon. Such a position would enable the spectator's eye to follow the course of the line through all its varying curves. For better definition the angler might wear light clothes and use a light-coloured rod against a dark background. The line, to render it more conspicuous, should be a thick one, and if it were parti-coloured, say a yard of white, a foot of black, a yard of white, and so on, it would show its progress along its course instead of appearing as a lengthening and shortening white streak.

I have no doubt that the majority of our fly fishermen have always cast their flies by various, to them nameless, methods they have picked up from brother anglers at the riverside, adapting to the requirements of the occasion such dodges and wrinkles as they have found out for themselves or adopted by observation from others, and doing it all in a casual, matter-of-fact way.

A famous veteran down-and-across wet-fly fisher once confided to me: "I've just been reading a book on fly fishing, and the chap has a lot to say about what he calls the 'Spey cast'; but I can't make head or tail of it. What the mischief *is* this Spey cast?" And, as gently as I could, I broke the truth to him that it was the identical cast he had been making as I came along the bank and the one he habitually employed when the conditions were suitable.

In his useful little book on *Fly and Bait Casting* R. D. Hughes, whose name is emblazoned large on the records of international casting tournaments, says, "I myself started fishing at the age of ten, and was fortunate enough to worry my way to a certain degree of effici-

ency without help. . . . Nearly thirty-five years passed
away before I seriously considered the principles which
guided me." My own case, and that of thousands more,
was somewhat similar. In the days of my youth, possessed
of my first fly rod, I made a few essays on the grass at
the overhead cast, the simplest form of the two-motion
cast, in which, with an almost vertical wave of the rod,
you fling the line behind you, pause a second or two to
allow it to extend fully in the rear, then fling it forward
with a vertical wave of the rod to the spot aimed at.
Finding I could manage this—in a fashion—without
entangling my line with the rod top or with itself, I
started out on my first fly-fishing expedition, and returned triumphantly with four half-pounders, all caught
on the March Brown. After that I just went on fly fishing whenever I had the opportunity, finding out things
for myself and—man is an imitative animal—copying,
to the best of my ability, the things I saw practised fly
fishers do without assiduous reference to the manual.

Practice with the overhead cast will serve to accustom
the muscles to their new job, and when the tyro has acquired confident control over the line's airy evolutions
he will, almost instinctively, tumble into the fundamental principles on which other casts are based. Thus:
To avoid entanglement the back cast should be made
a little to the right of the reverse path of the forward
cast, and this causes the end of the line to describe a
sharp curve—a sort of a blunt-nosed angle—at the point
where the back cast finishes and the forward cast commences. This is called a narrow entry, and the narrower
the entry, the easier it is to cast against the wind. If the
two paths of the line are wide apart, you get a broad
entry, against which the wind offers more resistance.
But curiosity, which leads to experiment, may prompt
you, when the wind is not against you, to make trial of

31

a broader and still broader entry, leading to the discovery that with a wide backward curve there is no necessity to wait for the line to straighten behind you, and you have unconsciously absorbed the underlying principle of the switch and other continuous-motion casts.

Or, as you proceed along the bank from one pool, say, to another, instead of reeling up and securing your fly or flies, you prefer to exercise your dexterity by making false casts in the air. From the simple to-and-fro motion of the overhead cast you advance to the more artistic figure-of-eight, and you have hit on a useful way of changing the direction of your cast.

Again, while fishing the ordinary overhead cast, a wind blowing from your right causes you some inconvenience, when it strikes you that an easy way to avoid this nuisance is by making the back cast to your left instead of to your right, with your forearm across your chest, and the forward cast over your left shoulder, and you have stumbled on the backhand cast.

Still again, for some reason or other—possibly through trying some original dodge for getting out a long line preparatory to making your initial cast—you find yourself holding your tail fly between the finger and thumb of your left hand, with fifteen yards or so of looped line trailing in the water. Obviously you have got to get that line into the air before you can make your forward cast. Naturally, the first thing to do is to raise the rod; but that is not enough to lift the whole of the line. Happy thought! Without a pause you swing the rod point away from you to the right—releasing the fly as you feel the pull on it—and commencing the swing with an easy dip that merges into an upward curve bringing the rod point to the perpendicular, and thence, as the line bellies out over the water in obedience to the rod, you make, again without pause, the forward cast. And, lo! you have acquired the essential idea of the Spey cast.

One of the difficulties in learning to cast "by the book" is due to the divergence of opinions held by the writers as to the correct methods of manipulation to produce the desired effects. For instance, at the very outset comes the question: How to hold the rod? R. D. Hughes says, "The main hold is with the four fingers only. The thumb is placed at the back of the rod—*i.e.* on the side opposite to the reel—while the fleshy part of the hand below the little finger is also against the back of the rod. The grip of the rod should be quite easy, not sloppy, but entirely devoid of any tenseness. If the rod is grasped tightly, a stiffness of all the muscles of the body results, and perfect freedom of every muscle and joint is required for throwing a fly as much as in all other games."

Now read what F. M. Halford wrote in his *The Dry-fly Man's Handbook*. "The majority of first-rate performers grip the rod (in the right or left hand), holding it tightly between the ball of the thumb and the second, third, and fourth fingers, using the forefinger for regulating the line and pressing the thumb firmly, pointing upwards, along the handle of the rod. Marryat gripped his rod with both thumb and forefinger pressed against the handle and pointed upwards. He had an abnormally long finger; possibly this was to some extent the effect of his peculiar grip. He always considered that this grip gave him a greater power of directing the line and fly with extreme accuracy. It is comparatively unimportant which grip is adopted by the tyro, but it is all-important that he should from the first learn to hold the rod as tightly as possible if he wishes to be a good hand at casting." And, again, referring to Marryat in his *Dry-fly Fishing in Theory and Practice*, Halford says, "Grasping his rod with a grip like a vice, he put forth all his skill in casting, so as—to use his own expression—to 'combine delicacy and accuracy in the first chuck'."

You could not well have views more diametrically opposed than these, and yet no one will impugn either Hughes's or Halford's proficiency in casting the fly, while, though it is over forty years since he passed away, the memory of George Selwyn Marryat is still revered as that of the most skilful fly fisher who ever threw a line on the South Country chalk streams.

I believe popular opinion to-day favours the easier grip advocated by Hughes. Personally, and independent of any outside opinion, at one time I fell into the way of using the grip Halford first describes in the extract I have quoted, and I cannot honestly say that I cast very much worse than the average fly fisher. My bent forefinger was held away from the rod, just "feeling" within the crook of it the line between the bottom ring and the reel. By this means I was more sensitive—or I imagined that I was—to the touch of a fish which was taking the fly under water. At the same time I do not recommend this grip to any angler who is not possessed of a powerful grasp, as it throws undue strain on the third, fourth, and little fingers.

Then, again, there are the sturdy sticklers for casting from, respectively, the wrist, the forearm, and the shoulder. Out of all this confusion of conflicting opinions, it seems to me, emerges the truth that it does not matter how you cast so long as you achieve the object aimed at. The casting dogmatists always put me in mind of the strictly orthodox golfer who, at the first tee, kindly and painstakingly explained to his opponent that his grip, and his swing, and his stance were all wrong, and that he could not possibly hope to make a golfer unless he got rid of all these faults—and then lost the round to the pagan by six up and five to play.

Within reasonable limits I hold that the way which, after he has become on intimate terms with his rod and its general capabilities, comes most "natural" to a man is the correct method for him to adopt, his wrist, fore-arm, and shoulder being ready, and willing, to work harmoniously with one another as they may be called upon.

I think I have read pretty nearly all that has been published in books on fly casting, with the result that I fully endorse the dictum that the art cannot be learnt solely from written instructions. Yet a few notes on the salient features of the various casts may prove helpful.

The OVERHEAD CAST I have already briefly described. The general action is very similar to that of the driver of a four-in-hand when he is gently encouraging—not flogging—his team. With an easy rhythm, the thong is flung backward slightly to the right (that, in fly-fishing parlance, is the recovery), and flung forward over the right shoulder (that is the delivery). But it is not thrashed downward; instead, as the forward impetus is exhausted, it falls caressingly on the shoulder of one of the leaders. The same in making the forward cast with the fly rod; if you aim at the spot on which you want your fly to alight, line and fly will come down with a splash. You direct your aim at a point in the air a little above the water, and allow the extended cast to fall softly on the surface in the approved manner of the thistledown. "Thrashing the stream" may be good poetry, but it is darned bad casting.

There is another point to guard. If you make the overhead cast, as you should, with a narrow entry, and commence the delivery without sufficient pause to allow the line to become extended behind you, you will hear an ominous crack, and "bang goes saxpence" in the shape of an expensive fly. On the other hand, if you pause too long, your line falls so low that the hooks catch in the ground vegetation, and a broken cast may result.

The BACKHAND CAST I have also described, and what I have just said of the overhead applies to that likewise.

The STEEPLE CAST is the old-fashioned orthodox means of avoiding getting your line fouled by trees, a steep bank, or other obstruction in your immediate rear. Instead of flinging the line behind you, as in the casts already indicated, you throw it up into the air with an upward lift of the rod, pause till it is extended above you, and make the delivery with a downward and forward stroke. Certainly with this cast you dodge the obstacles behind you, but you usually end with slamming line and flies on to the water with a pronounced splash. In such an emergency as the steeple cast was designed to provide for the more modern switch cast is usually resorted to; it does its job without advertising itself too insistently to the trout.

The HORIZONTAL or UNDERHAND CAST is, in the method of manipulation, practically the same as the overhead, only that it is made low down and parallel to the water. It is very useful for getting the fly under overhanging boughs, and also for cutting in under an opposing wind. Further, and what at first strikes one as curious, a dry fly can often be made to cock—*i.e.* sit daintily right side up on the water—more easily with an underhand cast than with the overhead. The delivery may be made either above or below the plane of the recovery. If above, the fly alights more softly; if below, the casting is easier against a wind.

The BACKHAND-HORIZONTAL CAST bears the same relation to the horizontal as does the ordinary backhand to the overhead. It is performed with the right hand across the body. It is not easy to acquire the knack of it; but once diligent practice has brought proficiency, by gradually lowering the plane of action from that of the ordinary backhand, it will be found very useful in casting, while standing on the bank, to reach a spot under that bank and to your right hand when trees render the ordinary backhand impracticable. The only alternative in such a case is ambidexterity.

This exhausts the list of the two-motion fly casts in general use, *i.e.* casts in which a distinct pause is made between the recovery and the delivery. There is, however, what might, perhaps, be called a one-motion cast known as the CATAPULT CAST or CATAPULT SWITCH. The name almost explains the method. It is not often used, but occasionally it may enable the angler, blessed with a fair share of luck, to reach a spot inaccessible by other means. Line is drawn off to, approximately, the length of the rod, which is held low, parallel with the water, and the fly gripped between the finger and the thumb of the left hand. The left hand is then drawn back until the rod forms a bow. When the pull of the bowed rod is considered sufficient, the fly is released and the elasticity of the rod launches it on its course assisted by a little backhand flick of the right hand. Accuracy of aim is not easily acquired, and it is advisable that preliminary practice on the lawn should be undertaken.

The continuous-motion casts are made without any pause from the moment the recovery of the line commences to that when the fly hovers above the water, although the speed may alter during the successive phases of the cast. And the line is "kept alive" during the whole of its evolutionary progress. The essential principle of the continuous-motion cast is the wide curve, in which there is no abrupt right-about turn in the path of the line to crack off the fly. Owing to its wide entry the continuous-motion cast is most easily performed with a following wind to assist it.

The SWITCH CAST is the most commonly employed of the continuous-motion casts, and is in two phases merging into one another. Commencing with the line extended in front, and the rod held in a horizontal position, the rod top is drawn back in an upward curve until most of the line is clear of the water; then, without pause, the rod top is brought round and over the right shoulder and the forward throw made, the aim being well above the water to allow the fly to fall gently.

The DOUBLE SWITCH is a little more complicated and involves the change over from a right hand recovery to a backhand delivery over the left shoulder, incorporating the principle of the Spey cast. It is commenced in the same way as the ordinary switch, but when the line is mostly clear of the water in the lift, the rod top is swung to the right, causing the line to belly in that direction. Then, as the rod top comes up, it is swung to the left, brought round over the left shoulder, and the forward cast made.

The SPEY CAST is little known on the South Country chalk streams, and, indeed, it finds no place in many trout fishing books. But, as one travels north, it is to be met with in daily use on the wide moorland rivers, and a very useful cast it is to the down-and-across wet-fly fisher. Commencing with an upward lift, when the rod top reaches the top of the lift, it is swung with a dip followed by an upward curve vigorously away to the right, the line following in a wide belly.

The rod top reaches its highest point in the swinging curve behind the right shoulder of the angler, and the forward throw is then made.

It is to be noted that in none of these continuous-motion casts does the fly go appreciably behind the angler, and rearward obstacles lose their terrors.

SHOOTING THE LINE was originally introduced as a means of adding a few yards to the length of the cast made, and for this purpose it is still employed in tournament casting. In actual fishing it was found that by shooting the line at the correct moment the flies could be made to alight more gently on the water, and it is now regularly practised, especially in dry-fly fishing, with that as its main purpose. A loop of line is drawn off and held away from the rod by the left hand, the loop being between the lowest ring and the reel. As the forward cast is being made, about the moment when the drive of the forward throw has got in its work and the rest of the forward course of the rod becomes a follow through, the line is released and allowed to run through the fingers, when, if the psychological moment is well chosen, the slack shoots through the rings. If released too soon the power to pull the slack is wanting; if too late the line between rod and fly falls in an untidy straggle.

DRIFTING DOWN is resorted to in dry-fly fishing when, by reason of the presence of trees or other impediments, a rising trout cannot be approached from below—only from a point higher upstream. This drifting down can be accomplished by getting within casting distance of the rise, getting out enough line to allow the fly to drift well past the fish, and casting down towards it, but at a point a yard or so above the level of the stream. As the fly hovers for an instant in the air before falling, the angler pulls in towards him, when the fly falls lightly in front of the fish with a yard or so of slack to allow it to drift over the trout without drag. If necessary the drift may be further lengthened by paying out line.

In wet-fly fishing the object of the angler is to lay a straight line between the rod top and the fly, for often the only indication of an underwater rise is a tug, and an instantaneous strike should be the response. This is impossible if a series of zigzags have to be straightened out first. And, moreover, the touch of the fish is not felt if the line is slack. Incidentally, in wet-fly fishing if the line lies in a regular curve owing to the bellying of it downstream by the current, both the touch of the fish and the strike are communicated along the curve owing to the water's resistance.

In dry-fly fishing, however, the case is different. If a straight line is thrown across the current to a rising fish in the slacker water beyond, the faster intervening stream at once commences to belly the line, and the floating fly is dragged obliquely across the current, instead of swimming down with it in a natural manner, and drag is the bugaboo of the dry-fly man. To avoid it in such circumstances it is necessary to cast a wriggly line, so that the current has to straighten out its contortions before getting a pull on the fly, during which interval, it is to be hoped, the fly has effected its purpose.

If the cast is to be made across, or across and slightly downstream, the procedure already described in dealing with drifting down may be used. Otherwise, the wriggle may be imparted by delaying the shooting of the line the fraction of a second—experience only will teach how much—and advancing the rod as the fly is on the point of alighting.

In both two-motion and continuous-motion casting, whether wrist, forearm, or shoulder be employed, it is the rod that should do the bulk of the work, the arm supplying the impetus and guiding the action, and it is only by *making the rod bend* that it can be induced to perform its office with credit to itself and the angler.

CHAPTER V

STRIKING, PLAYING, AND LANDING

IT is told of an aspiring young American angler that he
travelled a thousand miles in the hope that he might
be permitted to sit at the feet of a renowned fishing
Gamaliel, and learn of him the secret of his sensational
catches. And the Waltonian prodigy, hitherto chary of
dispensing information on his methods, took pity on the
youthful enthusiast, and divulged the secret in a nutshell—"When you get a bite, jerk!"

There you have the basic sum and substance of the
strike. All that now remains to be considered is how
and when to "jerk". On these points opinions vary
widely, with regard to dry-fly fishing especially. One
authority says, "More fish are lost from striking too
soon than too late", while another as confidently states,
"I think more fish are missed by striking too late than
by striking too soon". I fancy most fly fishers will agree
with me that the correct timing of the strike on one
river differs from the correct timing on another, and,
further, may be influenced by the size of the fly. Thus,
on the rapid streams of the North and of the West of
England, where the nimble trout come to the fly in a
touch-and-go fashion, you cannot, as a rule, strike too
quickly; on the more placid chalk streams of the South,
where the plethoric denizens suck in the tempting morsel
with the studied leisureliness of a bricklayer on day-
work, the tightening of the line may well be delayed a
second or two.

42

"Striking" is a misnomer, the correct action being a mere tightening of the line—a gentle, but firm, twitch —sufficient to force the point of the hook home over the barb. If the pull is too gentle you probably lose your fish; if too violent the fish not only gets away but carries off a portion of your cast as a souvenir. The natural tendency is to strike too hard, and should the angler be unable, in the excitement of the moment, to exercise the necessary restraint, his remedy lies in "striking from the reel". In such cases the reel should be furnished with a medium check, just easy enough to allow the fish to draw off line when it makes a headlong rush. Instead of being clasped to the rod by the fingers, the line is left quite free between the bottom ring and the reel. Then, when the strike is made, the restraint of the check is sufficient to drive in the hook, and any surplus energy is harmlessly expended in drawing line from the reel.

The strike is made, usually, by raising the point of the rod with a wrist movement, and the quick strike is most needed when fishing the submerged fly—either the wet fly or the nymph. In fishing across-and-down a tug is generally felt, while in fishing upstream the flash of a gleaming side beneath the ripples, or the sudden stoppage of the line may be the signal that a trout is sampling the fly, and the responsive tightening cannot be effected too quickly.

In spite of the modern fly rod, especially the dry-fly rod, possessing more backbone than its predecessors, and consequently being quicker in the strike, and in spite of the weight of the line acting as a curb to some extent on the natural inclination of the point to flop downward on applying the upward impetus to the butt, there is still a slight momentary pause before the rod top gets in its work on the rebound. This difficulty can be overcome by holding a loop of the line between the finger and thumb of the left hand—as is done in preparation for shooting the line—and twitching it back simultaneously with commencing the strike with the rod.

I have written of the usual manner in which the strike is made—with the wrist. A better way, in my opinion, is to adopt an outward, sideways motion of the arm, which decreases the amount of momentary flop in the rod top.

In fishing a typical chalk stream you can often watch the fish deliberately approach the fly in the clear water, and the temptation to strike too soon is great. You cannot fairly hook a fish until the fly is in its mouth.

Having hooked the trout, the rod should be kept well up, when the affair becomes largely a contest between the fish and the rod. Sometimes the rod is playing the fish, and sometimes the fish is playing the rod. The quarter-pounder of the moorland river may be dealt with summarily, and brought flip-flopping to the landing-net. Trout of heavier calibre may have to be humoured to the extent of allowing them to run off line in their panic-stricken rushes in water free from obstacles, though a steady strain is kept on them all the time. Such mad rushes have an exhausting effect on the fish, and it soon tires. The old veteran which steadily signalises its objection to being caught by solemnly and sedately moving to right and left in the depths like a sentry on his beat puts up a much longer, if less thrilling, argument.

A trout can generally be turned by putting a steady side strain on it, or when it is desperately heading for refuge, say, in a weed-bed, slacking the line will frequently deceive it into a false sense of freedom, and it will halt in its headlong career.

Of course, if the angler is fishing upstream every effort

should be made to bring the hooked fish down and play it out in the water below, so as not to disturb the fish higher up.

There is one point in connection with playing a trout on which, I am afraid, I am hopelessly unorthodox. I may be obtuse, but I cannot see the logic in, what is so often recommended by angling writers, dropping the rod point and giving slack when a hooked trout leaps in the air, in order, so it is stated, to avoid the fish's falling on the line and bringing about a smash or the tearing out of the hook. Far more reasonable, it seems to me, to keep a fairly taut line on the trout both in the water and out. The elasticity of the rod is sufficient to deal with the momentum of the upward spring and the gravity of the fall. Inevitably the trout must come out of the water head first, and the head is the point of its connection with your line. Once out of the water it has no power of resistance, and a pull on the line will keep its head towards you during the whole of its saltatory demonstration, with the result that the line is clear of its body when it falls. Anyhow, that has always been my practice, and I have had no reason to regret my adoption of it. Once for a brief instant I wavered in my faith when a big lake trout of 5 lb. or 6 lb. came unstuck on the completion of a magnificent leap; but an examination of the tackle quickly revealed the cause of the loss—a badly tempered hook had pulled out straight in the course of a prolonged fight, and, naturally, had lost its hold.

Having played out his fish, the angler's next job is to land it, and here again I find myself at issue with class-book instructions. I agree that it is folly to attempt to "scoop out" the trout with the net; the fish may be responsible for a contretemps which may defeat your purpose and give it its liberty. Instead, the net should be submerged and the fish brought over it, when net and

45

trout may be lifted out. But here is where we differ: It is commonly advised that the net should be submerged below the position of the trout in the stream, and the trout should then be allowed to drift down the current into the net, in which case it enters the net tail first—and, possibly, as the net is lifted, jumps out again.

The fish should be led into the net head first. It cannot then jump out. Its leaping power is in its tail, not its head. Even though the net be not large enough to accommodate the whole of a big fish, if the head and the bulk of its body are in the net it is in safe custody.

Landing a fish while wading may present difficulties to the novice. The following hints should remove them. On moorland streams there are commonly practised two methods, than which I have yet to discover a better. In either instance turn your back to the wind, so that the breeze blows your released cast away from you. If you are using a long-handled landing-net, spiked for use as a wading staff, after netting the fish thrust the butt of your rod, reel and all, down the top—inside, of course—of your right wader, it being assumed that you are wearing wading stockings. Then, thrusting the shaft of your net between your legs and against the bed of the river behind you, grip the upper end of the shaft between your legs above the knees. You have then both hands free, and can conduct further operations inside the net itself, which is immediately in front of you.

If you are using a short-handled net—and you can apply this method to the long-handled net as well—thrust the butt of your rod down the right wader as before. Then tuck the handle of your net under the left arm, and grasp your fish with the left hand *outside* the net, while you release your fly with your right hand inside the net. The net intervening between your left hand and the fish enables you to get a better purchase on the slippery customer.

Having unhooked your trout, you will in mercy spare it unnecessary suffering by promptly administering the *coup de grâce*, as described in Chapter III.

It may be that, with a view to further slaughter, you are curious to know the particular speciality in diet in which the fish you have just landed has been indulging. Formerly the pursuit of knowledge in this direction necessitated the performance of an autopsy. But since G. E. M. Skues discovered that it was possible, at one quick operation, to evacuate the trout's stomach and fill a long-felt want by scooping out the contents with a marrow spoon thrust down the fish's gullet, the messy business can be avoided.

CHAPTER VI

KNOTS

I T is essential that the novice should, before commencing operations on the river, make himself familiar with, at least, two or three simple knots useful in joining gut, attaching—if he be wet-fly fishing—his droppers to the cast, and attaching his cast to the reel line. And here it should be noted that the material he is dealing with, whether gut, gut substitute, or hair, should be thoroughly soaked in water before it is tied. Otherwise it will break when the knot is tightened. These materials are brittle when dry, pliable when saturated.

The tyro may shrink with dismay from the sight of some of the diagrams of complicated knots, occasionally recommended, that seem to combine all the windings and wiggles of the Gordian Knot and the Cretan Labyrinth. But let him take heart. There is no call for a scare. He may worry along very comfortably for years, perhaps for the whole of his angling career, with one knot, variously applied, and that knot the simplest of all—the knot the lady ties on the corner of her handkerchief as a safeguard against forgetting something.

Immured in a loathsome cell in the villainous prison at Marseilles, Mr John Baptist Cavalletto, with the assistance of a powerful imagination, gave the piquancy of variety to his monotonous chunk of coarse dry bread by cutting it "so, like a melon. Or so, like an omelette. Or so, like a fried fish. Or so, like Lyons sausage."

In somewhat similar fashion the angler treats the

simple knot—which is known as the overhand, or thumb, knot—so, with an extra turn before he threads the end through the loop, and he has a double overhand knot. Or so, and he has joined two lengths of gut together. Or so, and he has made a loop at the end of his cast. Or so, and he has a still better loop. Or so, and he has a Turle knot. Or so, and he has a fisherman's knot. Or so, and he has a half-hitch jam knot. Or so, and he has a barrel knot. In fact, there are very few knots known to the angler of which the overhand is not the fundamental principle.

OVERHAND, OR THUMB KNOT

Until our own times the means most commonly employed for joining two lengths of gut was the fisherman's

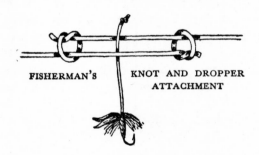

FISHERMAN'S KNOT AND DROPPER ATTACHMENT

knot. It is still very largely used, and for hair casts there is none better. On the end of one strand make an overhand knot, and, before drawing tight, pass through the loop formed the end of the other strand, on which make another overhand knot round the first strand. Then draw each knot reasonably tight and pull the two free ends in opposite directions, when the two knots will slide along until they jam against one another. This is a fairly reliable knot, and has the great advantage of providing the readiest method of changing a dropper when desired with the minimum of trouble. In making the knots the ends of gut or hair should not be cut off close after being drawn tight, but should be left to protrude an eighth of an inch. By taking hold of these ends and pulling, the two sections of the knot may be drawn apart and the knotted end of the gut or hair of the dropper inserted as shown in the illustration, when all is drawn tight again. In this way droppers may be attached at any joining in the cast. The majority of trout fishers do not make up their casts, but buy them ready made. In these the knots, professionally tied, and to be described later, do not admit of being drawn apart, and in such cases the knot may be cut out where it is wished to insert a dropper and the fisherman's knot substituted.

Another very easy way of joining gut strands is to use the double overhand knot. Lay the two strands parallel with a couple of inches or so overlapping; then, treating the overlap as a single strand, commence to make an overhand knot on it, but make an extra turn, as shown in the illustration, before putting the combined ends through the loop and pulling tight. This ensures a

DOUBLE OVERHAND KNOT

thoroughly reliable join, but it is rather bulky. It is one of the knots recommended for gut substitute.

A neater join is effected by a slight elaboration of the fisherman's knot, and this is sometimes called the barrel knot. It is in reality a double fisherman's knot, with a double turn taken over *both* strands before the end is slipped through the loop and drawn tight. This can be used in the same way as the fisherman's knot for the quick changing of knotted droppers. It is a safer knot than the single fisherman's when the two strands of gut

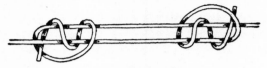

BARREL KNOT

to be joined vary considerably in thickness. It is also a good join for gut substitute.

Now, while the foregoing methods of joining gut will serve, and serve well, the safest and strongest knot of all for this purpose is the blood knot. I do not know who gave it that name, or why. Previous to 1910 the knot was known to a few anglers who were lucky enough to get hold of a cast in which it was incorporated, but the method of tying it, zealously guarded by the one or two in the secret, long and successfully defied detection. The leading tackle dealers could not produce it, and it remained a mystery until A. H. Chaytor, after much research and experiment, published the solution to the world in his *Letters to a Salmon Fisher's Sons*.

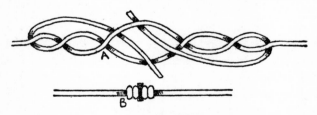

BLOOD KNOT

I cannot do better than quote Chaytor's own description, which the reader will easily follow with the aid of the illustration.

51

"(1) Lay the ends of the two strands of gut side by side as you wish to tie them and about one-eighth of an inch apart, holding them with your left hand, the end of the left-hand strand being nearer to your body.

"(2) With your right hand take the nearer end and wind it three times round the other strand (winding over and away from you).

"(3) Then bend the end back and poke it down between the two strands where your left thumb was.

"This is half the knot done: the other half consists in doing exactly the same thing with the opposite half of the knot.

"(4) Shift the half knot as it stands into your right hand.

"(5) Take the loose end and bring it *over* the strand towards you and so wind three times round the link of the gut.

"(6) Then bend it back and poke it upwards between the two links so as to lie beside the other loose end, but pointing the opposite way.

"Then, to pull the knot tight, slightly moisten the left finger and thumb, and with them hold the knot lightly whilst you pull the ends firmly and sharply. The knot will run up into a complete and translucent roll with the two ends sticking out at right angles, and they can then be cut off short."

Thanks to Chaytor and his classic work, the blood knot is now generally used by the professional tiers. The illustration shows, A, the principle of the knot, and, B, its appearance when completed.

Having proceeded thus far in preparing the cast, the next thing to be considered is the method to be adopted for attaching it to the reel line, and a start is made by tying the end into a loop. This is most easily effected by doubling the end of the cast and tying the twofold gut in an overhand knot at the spot where the base of the loop is to be. This is quite a good loop, but it leaves the

SIMPLEST METHOD OF LOOPING GUT CAST

loop forming an obtuse angle with the rest of the cast. I do not know that this materially affects one's casting, but it certainly gives the thing a cock-eyed look which can scarcely be described as æsthetic.

A more symmetrical effect can be achieved by making a simple overhand knot about two and a half inches from the end of the cast, bending back the end of the cast and bringing it through the bight of the knot before the latter is drawn tight,

BETTER WAY OF LOOPING GUT CAST

and making another simple overhand knot with the end of the gut round the main length of the cast. Pull all tight, sliding the last-made knot up to the other as you do so, and you have an attachment free from any bad alignment.

Next, having formed our loop on the cast, we have got

SIMPLEST ATTACHMENT OF LINE
TO CAST

to attach it to the reel line, and this can be done in a very simple manner. Make an overhand knot at the end of the reel line, then thread this under the loop of the cast, over one strand of the loop, under both strands, over the other strand, under the reel line, and over the strand of the loop first crossed. Pull tight, and as you do so cajole the reel line so that the knot at the end of it lies snug against the loop. This is a thoroughly reliable fastening—so reliable that thousands of anglers have used none other. But the objection is raised that, in wet-fly fishing, the knot on the reel line causes a slight disturbance when drawn through the water.

Any risk of this may be avoided by substituting the figure-of-eight knot, which requires no knot on the reel line, and leaves the short waste end lying snugly alongside the loop. The accompanying sketch gives a better idea of the ins and outs

FIGURE-OF-EIGHT ATTACHMENT
OF LINE TO CAST

of this knot than words of mine can convey.

There now remains the question of tying an eyed hook, whether a dry fly be busked thereon or not, to gut, and for the simplest, yet efficient, method of so doing generations of dry-fly fishers have risen up and called its inventor, Major Turle, blessed. In making the popular Turle knot, the end of the gut is passed through the eye of the hook, and then, below the hook, tied with an overhand knot round itself, forming a slip-knot. The hook, or fly, is then passed up through the loop of the slip-knot, and all is drawn taut.

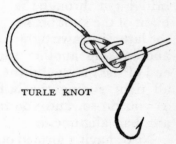

TURLE KNOT

For attaching gut to an eyed hook many anglers never use anything but the Turle knot. For very small flies, however, the half-hitch jam knot gives a tidier appearance. The principle of it is shown at A in the illustration. To achieve the result the end of the gut is passed down through the eye of the hook, and an overhand knot, as shown at B, made above it, with the hook hang-

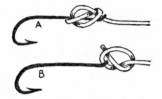

HALF-HITCH JAM KNOT

ing in the bight. Then, in drawing tight, the gut loop is wheedled over the eye, and pulled tight, when the knot arranges itself around the neck of the hook.

NOTE

To attach line or trace to a swivel, or trace or cast to lure or eye of hook, the Half Blood is recommended.

When using monofilament nylon this knot, perfected by Messrs Hardy, is an alternative.

To mount a trout fly on a monofilament cast this version of the Turle knot lies neatly, and is easily learned.

(The difference is that a double overhand knot, instead of a simple overhand, is used to form the running loop.)

For flies tied on hooks with a larger eye, as for salmon and sea-trout, this knot (another of Messrs Hardy's) is advised.

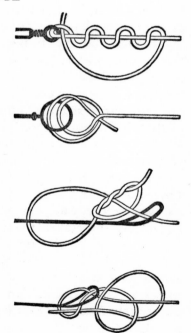

CHAPTER VII

WET-FLY FISHING

FLY fishing for trout is the art of presenting to the notice of the fish, with the assistance of a rod and line, a small hook so cunningly bedizened with silk and feathers, or other millinery materials, as to delude it into the belief that it is a living natural insect, or, at least, something good to eat.

In one respect fly fishing bears a close resemblance to Local Option, in that it leaves to the elector the choice of wet or dry. The wet fly is fished submerged, if only a few inches; the dry fly is fished daintily riding the surface of the water. The wet fly is mostly used on the moorland rivers, and "moorland" is used throughout this book as a convenient, and recognised, term to denote the rapid streams, common to the north and west of Britain, whose upper tributaries so often have their origin in the mountain heaths and the ling-clad fells, in contradistinction to the even-flowing placid chalk streams, such as are typical of the waterways of Hampshire beloved of the dry-fly fisher. Each system is best in its own sphere, and it is only by right of seniority that wet-fly fishing claims first attention.

The angler, having made wet-fly fishing his choice, is then faced with the question: Up or down? In the practical application of these terms a wide margin of tolerance is observed. The upstream fly fisher does not exclusively make his cast to a point directly above him, nor does the wet fly man aim at a spot directly below him. Rather are the terms held to indicate that the former practitioner commences his operations at the bottom of the water to be fished, and gradually works his way upstream, throwing his flies over the higher water before him, occasionally straight ahead, but more often than not up and, to a varying extent, across; while the latter makes his start at the top of the length and travels downstream, fishing the water below him, usually making his cast at right angles to the current, and allowing the stream to carry the flies downward and across to his own side (or directly below him if he be wading) in a sweeping curve.

Until the publication of Stewart's *Practical Angler* in 1857 downstream fishing was the common practice, although the upstream method was not unknown. Stewart, however, created something like a revolution among those anglers who imbibed their philosophy from the written word, while others who learnt their rivercraft at the waterside sturdily stuck to the tenets of the older school. The most telling argument in the upstream theory is the fact that fish lie with their heads upstream, and, therefore, are more easily approached from behind. But that is far from being the only factor to be considered, and the happiest—and most successful —fly fisher is he who, flinging dogmatism aside, readily adapts his methods, upstream or down, to the circumstances in which he is fishing.

Each method has its advantages and its disadvantages, but the upstream method is given the greater share of publicity in the Angling Press. Major Hills hits the mark in his *History of Fly Fishing for Trout* when he says, "Future students, reading the printed word, would imagine that from Stewart to now everyone fished upstream except some obscure individuals fishing untried waters. But that is historically untrue. Good fishermen, on the shyest of waters, fish downstream and kill fish. Their practice differs from theory, as it often does. Downstream fishing, here and now, in this twentieth century, is better for certain persons and certain occasions." All of which I heartily endorse, with the proviso that "Many" be inserted before "good", after having fished both up and down for more years than the great majority of men can count in their angling careers.

In striking, when fishing up, the hook is pulled towards some portion of the fish's mouth, which gives a better chance of its fastening; in fishing down the strike is made away from the fish's mouth, which lessens that chance. Against this is the fact that in fishing up many of the rises are imperceptible to all who do not possess the "sixth sense", and are, consequently, missed; while in fishing down every rise is either seen or felt, and instant response can be made.

In fishing down—and this is of special interest to the novice—an imperfect cast is speedily straightened out by the current.

In fishing up a short line is used and only a few yards of water can be fished at each cast. This involves almost constant casting, three or four throws being made for every one necessitated by fishing down. Thus the upstream flies pass a considerable part of their time in the air, whereas the downstream flies are fishing pretty nearly all the while, which is a material advantage if we are to accept Dickie Routledge's dictum. Moreover, however light may be the tackle, the constant casting entailed in fishing up is three or four times more fatiguing to the arm, and that counts in a long day's fishing.

In fishing a narrow stream—call it brook, beck, or burn—all the advantages lie with the upstream method, for there is no room for casting across, and to throw directly downstream is little better than useless.

Wading up against the current, even if it be no more than knee-deep, is very tiring to the legs, compared with the gentle movement down with the stream.

A point in favour of the upstream method is that, having hooked your fish, you play it out below the point of connection, and thus avoid disturbing the water still to be explored with your flies, while in fishing down you fight it out with the quarry in the very area, maybe, over which your flies are likely to pass at your next cast.

Then there is the wind to be taken into consideration, and that may be your deciding factor, for ceaseless slogging against the wind is a weariness to the flesh.

Now, take the case of a wide rippling flat with a gentle even flow. There is no visible fly on the water nor any indication of rising fish; but, for all that, the trout may be in the humour to take a submerged artificial. To search that flat with the upstream fly would be a long and, possibly, tedious process, while it could be combed by the downstream method in a fraction of the time.

Now comes the problem: With how many flies on his cast should the wet-fly man fish? This depends to some extent on circumstances. In fishing a sluggish river, such as the typical South Country chalk stream with its luxuriant weed beds, the safest plan is to confine oneself to one fly. Two flies—a stretcher, or tail fly, and one dropper—is rather risky, while to mount more than two is asking for trouble in the shape of entanglement.

Two flies are quite sufficient in fishing a small stream. Even then interesting little episodes are to be encountered. I had a friend who had the fishing on a lovely little trout stream, a capital stretch of which consisted of a series of small terraced pools, the water passing from one to the other over a shallow fall, and often, fishing with a couple of flies on my cast a yard or more apart, I have found myself playing two different trout in two different pools at the same time.

And let me say here that in the event of the angler having two or more trout on at the same time he should make a point of getting the one furthest from him into the net first, the one nearest to him last, otherwise he will find himself faced with a puzzle it may tax all his ingenuity to solve.

On the moorland rivers, whose gravel beds are swept clear of weed beds by the vigorous spates, more flies are commonly used on the cast. Three—one tail fly and two droppers—is the number most frequently employed on the wet-fly waters of the West of England and the Midlands. In the Northern Counties and over the Border four go commonly to the cast, and occasionally five are fished at once, while in days gone by one famous wet-fly man, with whom I frequently fished, often, when no sign of the natural fly was apparent, fished with as many as seven or eight on his cast.

"Let 'em think there's a hatch coming down", he was wont to chuckle, and certainly he caught fish with his entomological menagerie. Whether he would have caught as many if he had used only the customary quartette I cannot say.

Droppers are flies attached to the cast by short lengths of gut or hair at intervals of 18 in. or more, according to the number used and, to some extent, the positions of the knots in the cast. Some anglers vary the length of the attachment from 2 in. in the case of the dropper nearest to the stretcher to 4 or 5 in. in that of the top one, fishing the cast so that the top dropper trips lightly over the surface of the water, when it is called the bob or bob fly. This can be done in fishing a short line, and often proves very effective; but the majority of wet-fly fishers, especially across-and-down men, stick to a roughly universal standard of 2 in. to 2½ in. as more convenient; for then the droppers can be changed from one position to another, and, if the trout show a marked preference for one particular pattern, the cast can be mounted with flies of that pattern, to the exclusion of any other, without the necessity of carrying a lot of assorted lengths.

Droppers on fine gut have a pet weakness for entwining themselves lovingly round the cast, when the exhibition of a decided stand-offishness in their character would be far more agreeable to the angler. The man who fishes hair does not suffer from this source of irritation. Hair does not possess this clinging tendency; it is more independent, and stands boldly out from the cast. Even when fishing with a fine gut cast it is by no means a bad plan to mount it with droppers tied on single hair. In no case should droppers be used on gut finer than 3X, although the cast to which they are attached may be of 4X.

Of recent years there has been a marked tendency among wet-fly fishers to substitute flies on eyed hooks for the whipped-on patterns, and the change-over has proved a convenient and economic success in many respects, especially in the case of the tail fly. At the same time there are other fly fishers—and I am not quite sure that I am not one of them—who, while welcoming the eyed hook for the tail fly, prefer the whipped-on variety for the dropper.

The downstream fisher's typical opportunity comes when, after a rousing spate, the river has fined down to a nice bold water, its turbidity has given place to a clear "pale ale"—"sherry", if you want to be more polite—tint, and a refreshing downstream breeze strikes the pools and glides in a funny spot and stirs them into little laughing wavelets. There may be no sign of fly on the water, but the downstreamer does not let a trifle like that disturb his equanimity; the trout may be busy snapping up oddments in the bargain basement, as it were, and the business of the sunk fly is to seek them there.

The long line uncurls, more or less at right angles to the current, over the murmuring waters, and lightly drops its leash or quartette of flies athwart the stream. To avoid, or rather to delay as long as possible, the drag which sooner or later is exerted on the flies in this style of fishing may be desirable, but opinions differ as to the best means to be adopted to that end. Edmonds and Lee, in *Brook and River Trouting*, write: "The angler faces the bank towards which he purposes fishing, casts across and slightly upstream, then allows the flies to be carried without drag till they reach a point a few yards below where they alighted upon the water".

On the other hand Keith Rollo, in *The Art of Fly Fishing*, opines that, "Many Anglers who complain of their non-success when fishing down impart drag to their flies by casting too much upstream. . . . If you imagine twelve o'clock is straight upstream, and six o'clock is straight downstream, one is almost certain to get drag when fishing down, say, from two o'clock, but by casting at three-thirty the current will catch the flies at the right angle to allow them to float down naturally without drag. . . . You should always cast downstream at a point below the right angle."

Personally I do not believe that any general rule can be laid down as to the exact angle at which to make the cast across, as much depends on whether the water carrying the flies is running at a greater speed than the intervening water carrying the line, or vice versa. But this need not worry if the angler will cast approximately straight across, and follow the advice once given by

Sidney Spencer in the *Shooting Times*. Before making the cast, draw off one or two loops of line from the reel, and hold them with the fingers of the extended left hand, as when prepared for shooting the line; then gradually release these loops as is expedient, and so very materially lengthen the drift of the flies before the bellying line drags them out of their course.

At the worst the avoidance of drag is not nearly so important in wet-fly fishing as in dry-fly practice. The pampered gourmet of the placid chalk stream lolls at ease while the current places before him in orderly procession the epicurean dainties, which, even then, he has time to regard with a critical eye before sampling them. His knock-about brother of the moorland river has to work for his living on the dash-and-grab principle, as his items of fare are swept suddenly into the limited range of his vision, and rapidly swept out again unless he make a quick little dart to right or left. He has not time to be too critical, and, further, the eddies and divergencies caused by boulders, shouldering the flies this way and that, familiarise him with movements that the chalk stream connoisseur would esteem highly suspicious.

Most probably the angler will get most rises during the first few yards of the progress of his flies after their fall on the water, often almost at the very moment they alight, and such rises may cause a visible disturbance. At other times, especially as the pull of the line brings them sweeping round in a curve across the stream, the only sign and token of a rise will be a quick twitch of the line, to which instant response should be made. Even when the line is extended straight downstream a trout will sometimes take if, previous to making a fresh cast, the rod top is raised and lowered, sink-and-draw style, a few times. And in making the throw with a long line in this kind of fishing the Spey cast will be found very useful.

Though the whole width of the water may be negotiable from one bank, the man with waders will still have a decided advantage, seeing that, while one piece of water is best fished from the right bank, the next, for various reasons—say the run of the current or a fringe of bushes—may be unfishable except from the left bank, and the wader is able to cross over. Better still is the stretch of broad river, 30 yds. or more wide, which is fordable, for here the angler may wade down the middle, alternately throwing to right and left, as he moves down a yard or so at each cast.

Often the downstreamer will come to long pools, the beds of which shelve gently from a gravelly beach at one side to deeper and faster flowing water under the far bank, and this deeper current, frequently shaded by overhanging trees, the trout love to haunt. Here, from the shallow side, he will cast across well in towards the opposite bank, and allow his flies to swim down the deeper current, and if the fish are moving at all, he is pretty certain to reap his reward.

I particularly remember one such spot on which I could usually depend for getting a brace or two of trout. One day I was fishing there and had already secured a brace when the keeper came along the bank, and stopped for a word or two with me.

"You've had many a good catch in this pool," he observed, and I modestly owned the soft impeachment. "But you'll never make as big a catch here as we did early this morning," he went on.

"Oh, what was that?" I inquired.

"We took a drowned man out, and the corpse was in a very bad state of repair—looked as if it had been in the water a long time."

64

Fancy is a fickle jade; there is no accounting for sudden changes in one's pet inclinations, and, somehow, I did not seem to want to fish that pool any more just then. A little later I gave that brace of trout to a man I happened to meet. Like Sir Philip Sidney, I felt that his need for them was far greater than mine.

In fishing such waters as I have up to now indicated it is customary to "work" the flies by imparting a tremulous motion to the rod top to give the semblance of life to them, but when one comes to the boisterous water the rough-and-tumble of the stream will do all that is necessary in that direction.

Should there be surface food in evidence, and a cross wind blowing, then the angler is most likely to obtain his best results by throwing across towards the lee shore, whither the flies have been blown and the fish have followed them.

So much for the downstream method. Fishing the wet fly upstream is more difficult; indeed, it is the most difficult form of the sport I know, not even excepting dry-fly fishing (to which, in some respects, it bears a recognisable family likeness), for it calls for more acute perception, quicker action, and a more intimate acquaintance with the whereabouts of the trout under each and every varying condition. From the ocular evidence of the natural rise the dry-fly man knows just where his intended victim is; the upstream wet-fly man, during the major part of his operations, has no such guide, and is dependent on his knowledge of where the fish ought to be.

Wading is essential to success if the water is to be covered on any but the narrowest of streams, and even on the small brooks and burns it is in the great majority of instances the only means of approaching the fish unperceived.

The first precept of the upstream fisher is to use the shortest line that will enable him to keep out of sight of the fish, and the length of this will vary in accordance with the character of the water he is fishing. In the case of the rough rapid he need not have more line out than, say, one and a half times the length of his rod, and the latter may measure 10½ ft. With this short line he is enabled to fish his cast with the tail fly submerged and, at least, the top dropper, or bob fly, frolicking upon the surface.

In very rough streams he will find his best chance of a fish in the shallow edges of the current, and into these he throws, upstream and slightly across, raising his rod top as the current sweeps the flies back towards him, but not too hurriedly, or he will drag them. More often than not he will not see his fish as it touches the fly, nor will he feel it. The only indication of contact will be the momentary stoppage of the line, and the strike must be instantaneous, for the trout plays the game on the tip-and-run principle.

The little bays sheltered by miniature promontories are favourite lies, for in them the fish can rest in comfort, while ever on the alert to absorb what goods the gods may edge into their places of retirement, or to dart out and seize some tempting morsel as it is borne past by the faster water. So, too, are the tiny eddies behind upstanding boulders, where they employ the same tactics. The rapid runs between two boulders should always be fished carefully, as the natural food of a wider area above is concentrated in them, and the fish in the adjacent eddies are often eagerly on the lookout for it. Such runs should be fished with short quick casts, four or five of them, before the spot is abandoned as hopeless.

Usually good holding water will be found at the tail of a pool, where, over the shoaling bed of the river, the waters gather into a glassy glide for their headlong plunge down the rugged chute. Here the stream is much wider, and every yard of it should be carefully searched, commencing with the water under the nearer bank and working gradually across to the opposite side; then moving upstream a yard or two, and working back, crossing and recrossing again and again. This does not make for rapid progress up the river, but it is well worth while.

Here, too, in the smooth water, a longer line must be fished, and that means increased difficulty in detecting the touch of the trout; indeed, the longer the line, the harder it is to spot the all but imperceptible pause— often quite imperceptible to the novice. More than one angling writer has described the ability to discern the moment a trout takes you under water as the "sixth sense". It can only be cultivated by long practice, when it becomes a sort of intuition. In some veterans of the craft it is developed to such an uncanny degree as to recall the instance of the bishop in the back blocks of Australia, who happened to encounter a stock drover at a moment when, in a fit of exasperation, he was pouring out a flood of profanity in one long-sustained cataclysm. Aghast, the bishop gasped: "I—I know it is my duty to reprimand you severely for the use of such language; but—but all I can do at the moment is to ask you how, and where on earth, you learnt to swear like that?" Whereupon the drover modestly replied: "Guv'nor, you can't learn—it's a gift!"

To the tyro the "sixth sense" may look like that, but appearances are deceptive. Some men may, and do, acquire the knack of striking at the correct moment more readily than others; but it is *not* a gift, and you *can* learn. Further, the angler of to-day has advantages the old-timer did not possess; he can furnish himself with a light-coloured line, and, taking a leaf out of the dry-fly man's book, he can grease that line to make it float, so that it is easily perceptible. The rest is a matter of continual and concentrated observation. At the moment there recurs to me an occasion when I caught, in unbroken sequence while fishing the wet fly upstream, 23 trout, not one of which broke the water, showed a flash in the water, or in any other way gave the slightest indication of its interest in my flies beyond the merest suspicion of a hesitancy in the progress of the line.

Gravelly shallows with a gentle flow of water over them are well worth exploring with a, for upstream fishing, longish line cast up and across. The run under a willow-fringed bank is pretty certain to hold a good fish or two; so is the water just below the point where a tributary brook contributes its quota to the commissariat of the main stream; and in the heads of the pools good trout are wont to lie in wait for what bounties the stream above may wash down to them.

Among the wet flies in general use may be mentioned the March Brown, Greenwell's Glory, Red Spinner, Alder, Governor, Grannom, various Olives, Green Drake, Grey Drake, Red and Black Palmers, Tup's Indispensable, Coachman, Hare's Ear, Sedges, Cinnamon Sedge, Olive and Red Quills, Coch-y-bonddu, Olive Dun, Iron Blue Dun, Black Gnat, Yellow Dun, Wickham's Fancy, Pheasant Tail, Silverhorns, and Sand Fly.

But various fishing districts have their own special patterns in popular use, and for use on Scottish streams a selection from the foregoing should be augmented by the addition of the Black Spider, Blae and Black, Blae and Silver, and Teal and Black.

To the fly list the North of England, and especially

"WILL THE TROUT TAKE IT?"—page 76

BROOK FISHING

Yorkshire, contributes generously, the bulk of the patterns being sparsely hackled, and popularly known as "Yorkshire Flies". They are in common use throughout the Northern Counties and on the Border rivers. The greatest favourites are: Winter Brown, Water-hen Bloa, Dark Snipe and Purple, Snipe Bloa (*alias* Snipe and Yellow), Orange Partridge, Yellow Partridge, Dark Watchett (hackled form of the Iron Blue), Brown Owl, Dark Needle, and Poult Bloa.

The West Country (Devon and Cornwall) specialises on the Half Stone, Blue Upright, Red Upright, Blue Quill, Rusty Blue, Yellow Badger, and Rusty Red.

Derbyshire, of course, is the home of the various Bumbles, Honey Dun, Furnace, Mulberry, and Yellow. But, while these are fished, more or less for trout, they are, perhaps, better known as grayling flies.

Dressings of, and notes on, the flies mentioned here will be found in Chapter XXIV.

CHAPTER VIII

DRY-FLY FISHING

THE object of the dry-fly fisher consists in the presentation of a cunningly devised artificial floating upon the
surface of the water, and doing it as to the manner born
with, apparently, such sweet ingenuousness that the
most hypercritical trout is lured into the fatal belief
that it is, say, some natural dun, perkily riding a-tiptoe
the bosom of the stream, as it dries its wings after emerging from the shuck and before taking flight.

Dry-fly fishing possesses a power of fascination over
its enthusiasts unshared by any other form of fly fishing,
due, I think, largely to the innate hankering in human
beings to "see the wheels go round". In wet-fly fishing
what takes place at the critical juncture is mostly
hidden from the eye; in dry-fly fishing it is, literally, all
on the surface.

It is not my purpose to trace in detail the development and spread of the dry-fly cult, suffice it to say that,
cradled on the South Country chalk streams, that steal
in gentle dalliance through the lush water meadows
and bosky arbours—streams in which fat trout lie in
the lap of luxury in the water aisles between the aquatic
weed beds while fairy flotillas of dainty duns sail down
the slumberous tide for their delectation—dry-fly fishing was in a bygone generation regarded by the great
majority of trout anglers as the amusement of a few
earnest, but misguided, crack-brains, and totally unfitted
for application to what were known as wet-fly rivers.

Gradually, however, the unbelievers were in increasing numbers brought to the penitents' bench, and to-day it is widely recognised that there are portions of all our rivers on which the dry fly, perhaps with little adaptations, may be successfully fished. As an instance of what may be done with the floater on water supposed to be utterly impossible, I mention the experience that befell a friend of mine, a skilful exponent of the dry-fly art, on a Scottish burn a few years ago. The water was low and clear, the sun riding the heavens in undimmed splendour. My friend let fall some observation touching his intention to try the burn with the fly, and the gravest suspicions were at once aroused with regard to his complete sanity. But when, in the face of the most earnest assertions of the local oracles, in whom was concentrated all knowledge, that under such conditions as then prevailed no possible blandishments whatever, save the clear-water worm fished well upstream, could prevail upon the mountain burn to yield up its trout—when, I say, my friend announced his intention to try the *dry* fly, suspicion as to his lack of mental poise became certainty in this overwhelming demonstration of sheer madness.

A mere Southerner to come over the Border to teach a Highlander how to sup brose! That was what it amounted to, and the local champion significantly observed that *he* purposed fishing a neighbouring burn with the worm. In short, the affair resolved itself into a match—Dry Fly *v.* Upstream Worm. Scrambling up the bed of the stream, and fishing with his single oiled fly each rocky pool before him, the dry-fly Southerner showed up at eventide with 34 trout against the expert wormer's 27, and Bannockburn was avenged.

For dry-fly work a heavy, double-tapered, water-proofed silk line is employed. This is necessary for casting against the wind. and to drive that line a more powerful rod than that usually used in wet-fly fishing is requisite. Of late years there has been apparent a tendency to shorten the length of the rod, and weapons of 8 ft. have had a certain amount of vogue; but the average dry-fly fisher will find 9 ft. 6 in. a convenient length.

To prevent its sagging and drowning the fly, and also to render it easily picked up, the line should be made to float, which is accomplished by a rubbing with a form of grease not readily washed off. In former days red deer's fat was the orthodox lubricant, but that has fallen into disrepute; so has petroleum jelly, both being under suspicion of having a deleterious effect on the line. Probably the most generally used flotant to-day is Mucilin, though there are many excellent specialities put up by the leading tackle firms. A readily available, and excellent, medium is common mutton suet, and I had one friend who persisted in using nothing but raw bacon fat. I had an uneasy feeling that the materials used in curing the bacon might have a ruinous effect on the line, but his lines gave long service. There is, however, one drawback to the bacon dressing—it requires to be renewed much oftener than other methods necessitate. With a good lubricant a good dressing before commencing fishing and one more at half-time should suffice to see one through a reasonable long day's sport.

Whether or not the gut cast should be greased is a question on which experts differ. Many practitioners leave the cast entirely ungreased, taking care to wipe off any lubricant that may have got on it accidently either from the reel line or the oiled fly. Others grease the upper portion of the cast, and leave 2 ft. or so next to the fly ungreased. The greasing may be effected by drawing the cast three or four times through a rag charged with Mucilin.

Now we come to the anointing of the fly. For the purpose of endowing the fly with such buoyancy as can be given it in the dressing it is hackled, pretty generously, with a feather from the neck of a cock, *Gallus domesticus*, varieties of which are bred for this special purpose. The hen's hackles are soft and quickly become waterlogged, while the cock's are stiffer and less absorbent. Still, even with the aid of frequent false casts made through the air, the fly would rapidly lose its buoyancy without auxiliary aid. This is customarily afforded by a touch of paraffin. A simple contrivance consists of a small bottle, containing the liquid, into the smaller end of the cork of which is inserted a feather. A bit of string tied round the neck of the vial provides a ready means of attaching it to a buttonhole. For many years I have had in use an excellent brass oiler with a screw top marketed by Cummins, of Bishop Auckland.[1]

At first ordinary paraffin was used, but, in view of the possibility that the trout might not like the pronounced flavour, many anglers changed over to the use of the deodorised variety. Apparently, however, the trout were indifferent to the change and a considerable reversion to the cruder quality followed. Within my knowledge one successful dry-fly fisher merely souses his fly well overhead in common paraffin, gives it a dabble in the water to wash off surplus, makes a couple of false casts to rid it of any globules of water it may have lifted, and proceeds with his fishing. In place of paraffin a liquid Mucilin is available, and many fishermen adopt the plan of smearing the fly with the semi-solid Mucilin and squeezing it between a rag.

I quote the following from that valuable angler's vade-mecum, *Where to Fish*:—"A method of making flies very buoyant is to soak them for some hours in the

---

[1] Now of Darlington.

paraffin oil as sold for fishermen, and then to let them dry completely. Another method is to dissolve a little petroleum jelly in some petrol and dip the flies into it. After the petrol has evaporated from the flies a thin coating of petroleum jelly adheres to them, and they can thus be carried ready for casting."

When the fly became waterlogged it was the practice to cast it backwards and forwards in the air until dry, before re-oiling it. This irksome process, or much of it, can be obviated by pressing the fly against amadou (if you are lucky enough to be able to get some), a fungus which has a wonderful absorbent power. Also when a fish has been caught, the fly, after removal, should be washed in the river to rid it of the fish slime, and pressed in amadou. Again, this valuable time-saver is brought into service when the line shows signs of losing its power to float. Before it is re-greased it is necessary that it should be dried, and a rub-down with the accommodating fungus will do the job, though to ensure thorough drying it is just as well, if the day be bright and sunny or dry and breezy, to stretch it for a short time in the open.[1]

A day in later May on a Hampshire chalk stream! The countryside, woodland and water meadow, is clothed in its fairest, freshest greenery, relieved here and there with fragrant clouds of hawthorn blossom and splotched with the golden gorse that is never out of bloom except when kissing is out of favour. The yellow iris, too, is already flaunting its flaming *fleur de lis* among the waterside vegetation. A gentle sou'-west zephyr breathes the promise of glorious summer to come. Silently and sleepily the river moves onward to its bourne, clear as crystal over its patches of gravel. Overhead the peaceful landscape is spanned by a vault of

[1] The use of one of the newly-developed silicone flotants renders such operations unnecessary, as these preparations make a fly more or less permanently waterproof.

blue, flecked and dappled with fleecy white. The weeds have been judiciously cut, so that the fishable water is not confined to narrow lanes between aquatic jungles.

If the angler is to restrict himself to dry-fly fishing pure and simple, there is no call for early attendance at the riverside, as the hatch of fly is not likely to come on until well into the forenoon. Probably a couple of hours before noon and a couple after will cover the period of the rise. Assuming an inconspicuous attitude he puts on the matutinal pipe, and waits, keeping an observant eye on the water. At first there is no sign of hatching fly or moving fish, but by and by a solitary dun, with its upright wings and dainty upward-arched body, comes floating saucily past. Soon others follow in straggling procession, and with the aid of the close-meshed landing-net the angler is enabled to scoop one out for examination. It is most likely to be one of the Olives, and an inspection of the fly boxes reveals a reasonably close imitation which is tied on the cast and anointed.

And now the hatch is coming down, not in single spies, but—well, if not in battalions, at least in platoons, and the trout apparently awaken to the fact. Probably they have during the first stage of the hatch been feeding under water on the nymphs as they rose from the bed of the river, and have been gradually led by them to the surface, where, by lying poised just below that surface, they can suck in the delectable morsels as they are borne to them without troubling to hunt them. Yonder, in mid-stream, a set of spreading rings betrays the position of a rising fish. The rings fade, only to be replaced by a fresh set diverging from the same centre. The phenomenon is repeated, a sure sign that the fish is steadily on the feed.

Keeping low, perhaps in a devotional attitude, the angler works out line by making false casts in the air,

75

until he has out what length, in his estimation, will suffice to reach a point a foot above the neb of the quarry. Then he makes his cast, only to find that his fly has fallen a yard short, and is ignored. Lengthening his line, he casts again—up and across, so that the gut shall not pass over the fish. This time the fly alights at the spot aimed at, but, alas! he has not thrown enough slack to allow it to drift down a few feet without a pronounced drag, and the fish's suspicions are aroused. A few false casts follow, to dry the fly and, perchance, allay the aforesaid suspicions. The third cast lays the gut slick across the trout's nose, puts it down, and the subsequent proceedings interest it no more.

The avoidance of alarming the fish is one of the first aids to successful dry-fly fishing. Remember the encouraging reply of the river-keeper to the novice who sought his opinion as to whether he was making any progress: "Well, I can't honestly say that you're catching more, but I think, if anything, you're scaring less".

Ah, well, a bad beginning often leads to a good ending, and our angler now moves unostentatiously up the bank a few yards until he spots another feeding trout. A long cast is required here, but a happy combination of skill and luck drops the fly, softly and well cocked, precisely at the point where it is likely to do most good, while at the same time the line falls with just sufficient zigzag in it to permit the tiny argosy to sail, "stately and swanlike", over the recently disturbed area. For one tense second everything else in the whole wide world fades into insignificance beside the all-absorbing problem: Will the trout take it? It will! The fly disappears in the centre of a beatific dimple, and for the next couple of seconds all the angler's powers of restraint are called upon to repress the instinct to strike too soon.

RESERVOIR FISHING

A Good Dish from Loch Leven—page 107

Having securely hooked his fish, the angler fails to pull its head at once downstream, and the panic-stricken trout, refusing to be hustled, makes a determined effort to seek freedom in the tangled depths of a near-by weed bed that has been left uncut to serve as a food factory. Nearer and nearer it wins to the longed-for sanctuary, when the angler, as a forlorn hope, suddenly relaxes the strain on the line. The dodge works. Momentarily lulled into a mistaken feeling of restored liberty, the fish ceases its struggle for the weed bed and turns its head upstream, when, with a steady side strain, it is worked into the more open water, and, by and by, over the ring of the landing-net—a gleaming, glorious 2-pounder.

Once a trout has buried itself in the fastnesses of the weeds there are three courses which may be pursued: You may slacken the line and possess your soul in patience until it comes out again of its own accord, trusting to luck that it may bring your cast and fly with it; you may, from a point lower downstream, put on it with the rod enough pressure to keep it kicking, on the chance that it may kick itself clear; or you may hand-line it, starting with a gentle steady pull, and gradually increasing the amount of tug until either the trout emerges or your line comes back sans fly, sans fish, sans everything.

So, picking up a good trout here, returning an undersized one there, and putting down several more, our angler may find himself with three or four brace, averaging $1\frac{1}{2}$ lb. apiece, in his creel when the hatch finally peters out and the floating fly's occupation, according to the tenets of the old-time Purists, has gone until the evening rise.

The Purists, at whose idiosyncrasies we love good-naturedly to gibe in these later days, abode by a stern

and unrelenting creed of Thou-shalt-nots.—Thou shalt
not fish anything but the rise, and that with a single
fly floating on the surface after undergoing the solemn
rite of anointment, and that fly as exact an imitation
of the natural insect on the water at the time as human
ingenuity can devise. Thou shalt not cast in any direction but upstream, save that the cast may be made upstream and somewhat across. There were other minor
Don'ts that I have forgotten. Anyhow, these dear old
Spartan boys would have let the wolf of keen desire
gnaw their vitals rather than that they should be guilty
of a breach of the faith, although I have heard of one—
possibly *ben trovato*—so far fallen from grace as to permit
himself to be discovered in the act of angling with a
plebeian worm, who sought to mitigate the heinousness
of the crime with the assurance that, at any rate, he
always oiled the worm first and fished it dry.

A wider tolerance now prevails. Even on what were
the most sacrosanct of dry-fly waters it is permitted, in
"prospecting", to "fish the water" in the hope of
attracting a fish when no rise of fly is apparent. There
has been a marked departure from the exclusive use of
the "exact imitation", hackled flies and "fancies"
which have no recognisable likeness to anything on
earth or in the waters under the earth being constantly
fished. Two flies on the same cast may be, and often
are, mounted; and, on occasion, the cast is not only
made down and across, but directly downstream and
drifted over the fish.

Still, while we may laugh at the narrow prejudices
of the Purists, let it never be forgotten that to these
pioneers we owe the establishment in our midst of an
engrossing form of angling that, in the opinion of many
thousands of its devotees, surpasses every other branch
of the sport.

It is in the application of the main principles of dry-fly fishing to rapid rivers that the departures from the original strict code are most noticeable. On the moorland rivers, so scarce are the hatches of fly as the South Countryman understands them, that the angler might wait—well, almost on "Kathleen Mavourneen" lines, "it may be for years, and it may be for ever". Of course, on the odd occasions when the fish are visibly rising and the object at which they are rising is apparent, he puts on his nearest imitation, and fishes that. Otherwise he mounts the fly that he thinks most likely to tempt the under-water feeder to rise to higher things. He may put on two flies of different patterns a couple of feet apart, nay, he may even put on a wet fly as stretcher and a dry fly as dropper as a means of ascertaining which is the more acceptable. One of my friends, who haunts the Border rivers in his spare time, is so unorthodox as to use persistently a submerged line when fishing the dry fly—says, with some reason, that it enables him to strike quicker—a practice which led one spectator to inquire sarcastically: "Are you a dry-fly fisher, or do you fish the fly dry?"

The quick strike is necessary in these rapid waters, as the fish do not lie immediately below the surface and leisurely suck in the gay deceiver; instead they come with a boil, and the response should be instantaneous.

Most of what I have written about fishing the wet fly upstream is equally applicable to dry-fly work. Practically all the water may be fished except the roughest streams, though in fishing the streams with the short line the fly is borne so swiftly over the few yards that are fishable that almost continuous casting is called for, and a spell with the longer line on the slower glides may come as a welcome rest. There is, however, this to be said of fishing the streams—drag is by no means so fatal to success as on the smoother stretches.

It is during the height of summer, when the moorland rivers have shrunk to the ghosts of their earlier selves, that the dry fly shows itself incomparably superior to the wet pattern, for by its skilful use many a nice dish of fish may be secured what time the wet fly would be little better than useless.

I have referred briefly to the changes that have been wrought in the matter of dressing the dry fly. When the present century was still young, F. M. Halford, who did more than any other man to set the new cult on a firm foundation, brought out, as the result of monumental patience, close observation and untiring research, the "Halford" series of dry flies. To the eye of the angler handling them they appeared to be the closest imitations of the natural insect the fly-dresser could ever hope to achieve, and they were eagerly accepted by the faithful. But in such matters as these the trout are the final arbiters, and their verdict in the case of many of the patterns was unfavourable. The majority of Halford's dressings have fallen into desuetude.

Halford viewed his flies from above through the air, while the fish view them through the water from below. Gradually our fly-dressers came to adopt as far as possible the trout's point of view, and, consequently, the hackled pattern, minus wings, came more into favour. What was the use of the wings, however close their mimicry, if the trout could not see them? And, obviously, when the fly was viewed from below, the body and hackles hid them. Their only mission of utility, when set on V-shaped, was to act as a parachute and ensure the fly falling on the water right side up. But, then, in the hackled pattern there is no wrong side up, all sides being alike, so what was the use of the wings at all? As indicating the extent to which the use of the hackled pattern has grown, it is worth noting that, as Major Hills has recorded in his *River Keeper*, "Excluding spent spinners, all Halford's patterns are winged. . . . Of Lunn's forty patterns only sixteen are winged." And both may be regarded as, in their respective days, the leading authorities on the world's most famous dry-fly river, the Test.

In 1924 the publication of J. W. Dunne's *Sunshine and the Dry Fly* (A. & C. Black, Ltd.) marked the arrival of a new principle in the dressing of dry flies. The author had noticed that, upon the application of oil, the body of the fly seemingly turned black, and on investigation found that what really happened was that the oil rendered the silk of the body translucent, and this allowed the darkness of the hook to show through it. Experiment proved that if the shank of the hook were first enamelled white, wrapped with coloured artificial silk, and then oiled, a coloured translucent effect was produced which closely resembled that of the natural fly when seen through the water from below. On this basis he worked out a series of what are popularly called "Sunshine" flies. These attained a wide vogue, and would be supplied by many of the leading tackle dealers.

Another modern style of dry fly is that invented by the late Dr Wm. Baigent, and, on his own authority, it was christened the "Variant" for him by his angling friends, quite independently, I believe, of the fact that, as H. D. Turing has reminded us, the name had already been applied to a fly invented by Horace Brown, a familiar figure on the Kennet. The leading characteristics of the two flies are, however, different, Horace Brown's fly consisted of a hackle tied on a bare shank, while the leading feature of the Baigent Variant, which is now the fly usually meant by that designation, is a bodied fly wearing a long sparse hackle. It is produced in various patterns, such as the Red, Rusty, Dark, Light, and Black. These have proved killers on all our dry-fly rivers.

One of the most conspicuous novelties in dry flies is Alexander Martin's "Parachute" fly. It is dressed mostly in hackled patterns; but the hackle, instead of forming a vertical *cheval de frise* round the neck of the fly, lies in a horizontal halo immediately above it, and does every credit to its name by causing the fly to fall on the water as softly as the proverbial thistledown.

In view of the wide range from which to select, and local predilections for certain patterns, the compilation of a list of the best dry flies seems to me a hopeless task; but I think that no dry-fly fisher's "favourite choice" would fail to include at least some of the following patterns: Dark Olive Quill, Gold-ribbed Hare's Ear, Greenwell's Glory, Ginger Quill, Red Quill, Orange Quill, Iron Blue Dun, Blue-winged Olive, Blue Upright, Red Upright, Pheasant Tail, Red Spinner, Dark Variant, Light Variant, Rusty Variant, Wickham, Small Sedge, Big Red Sedge, Coch-y-Bonddu, March Brown, Tup's Indispensable, and Black Gnat.

Dressings of, and notes on, the flies mentioned here will be found in Chapter XXIV.

CHAPTER IX

ARTIFICIAL MAY-FLY FISHING

"Boston?—Boston? Let me see, Boston's in America, isn't it?" casually observed a mere Britisher in the presence of a haughty lady from the U.S.A.'s centre of fashion and culture, who indignantly squashed him with: "Sir, Bawston *is* America!"

Similarly, we have in England anglers—there used to be more of them—to whom May-fly fishing *is* trout fishing, and no other branch of the sport is of any account: just as, in many parts of Scotland, the only "fush" is the salmon, and the trout is simply an "also swam".

On such rivers as provide a good rise of the Green Drake the May-fly season, which usually commences about the end of May and may be prolonged to the middle of June, is a period of gluttonous gorge for the trout, so that it is frequently styled the "May-fly carnival"; while, during that same period, the trout may so recklessly abandon their customary caution in the course of their gastronomic orgies that it is also known as the "duffers' fortnight". At this season the wily old patriarchs, at other times proof against the fly fisher's most cunning stratagems, fling themselves into the revels with the foolhardiness of untutored youth.

It was the custom of angling writers of a past generation to expatiate on the dense clouds of Drakes disporting themselves over the chalk streams of the South. Indeed, I have heard of the fly being so thick in the air in one district that the local train service could only be carried on with the aid of fog-signals, but I always regarded that statement, like the premature report of Mark Twain's death, as "greatly exaggerated". It is, however, the general opinion of to-day that of later years the May-fly rise has considerably diminished; in fact, it has entirely disappeared from some of the South Country rivers. This phenomenon is not universally regarded as a great calamity, and many are in entire agreement with Viscount Grey of Fallodon, when he says, in his *Fly Fishing*: "May is a good month on a chalk stream, but to my mind the perfection of dry-fly fishing is to be had on a good day in mid-June, on water where the May-fly never appears, first to excite the trout and the anglers, and then to leave the fish without appetite and the angler too often discontented. The May-fly is a fine institution, and where it comes in enormous quantities, as it does on some rivers such as the Kennet, which have but a poor rise of duns, it provides a fortnight of most glorious fishing; but elsewhere it interrupts the season, and unless the trout are very large, or where there is a great lack of duns and small flies, I would not attempt to re-introduce the May-fly where it has ceased to exist in any numbers."

In other words, after a surfeit of May-fly the trout lie low and fly fishing is practically at an end until the reawakening in September; whereas with no May-fly, sport with the smaller fly is possible throughout the summer. The fly fisher, in his choice of water, with respect to its May-fly rise or its absence of May-fly, is pretty much in the position of the small boy with his spoonful of jam. He may spread it over his slice of bread to give a delicate sweet savour to the whole, or, hankering after the sensational, he may gulp it down in one delicious dollop and worry through the remainder of his uninteresting fare as best he may.

The May-fly is far more widely distributed on our rivers than many suppose. It is very abundant on the Derbyshire streams. David Foster wrote in his *Scientific Angler*: "Nowhere have we had such sport with this fly as on the Dove. Centuries ago this river was considered the best stream for trout fishing in England, and it still bears the palm for Drake fishing." It, along with its neighbouring streams, still produces the May-fly in abundance. Another famous May-fly stream is the Costa, a sort of miniature Test in Yorkshire surroundings, and there are capital rises on the Upper Derwent and its bunch of tributaries in the Helmsley and Kirbymoorside districts. On these waters the appearance of the Green Drake is eagerly looked for.

There are hundreds of streams of the moorland type on which the Drake rises in considerable numbers, and yet the trout evince little or no interest in it—so little, indeed, that local angling writers—*e.g.* Edmonds and Lee, and F. M. Walbran—make no mention of it in their chapters on fly fishing.

It is characteristic of the trout of what we may regard as May-fly rivers that they show little inclination to rise during the first appearance of the Green Drake. I have often heard it hazarded that it takes them a day or two to re-acquire a taste for the toothsome morsel. I think the more likely reason is that at this stage the fish are feeding belowstairs on the nymphs as they emerge from their burrows or commence their ascent to the surface for their transformation act to the sub-imaginal stage. Later, perhaps in a couple of days, when the surface is dotted with the "greenery-yallery" sails of the animate fairy barks, the rise of fish comes on in earnest, the water is alive with spreading rings, and here and there an impetuous trout comes at the fly of its choice with a resounding wallop.

It is advisable on the South Country chalk streams, where there is always the chance of coming to grips with a 3- or 4-pounder while the May-fly is on, to increase the strength of one's cast to, at least, fine undrawn gut; but on other waters where the biggest fish that may be expected is an occasional pounder 2X drawn gut will be found quite thick enough.

Briefly, there are three phases in the life-cycle of the May-fly with which the angler is mostly concerned— the nymph stage during the period from its emergence from its burrow in the mud or silt on the stream bed to its arrival on the surface of the stream; the sub-imago stage, during which, having crept out of its husk and assumed the winged form, it rides the water daintily as the Green Drake, while its wings dry sufficiently to bear it aloft and carry it landward to shed a further skin and appear as the imago, or perfect insect. The female is then known as the Grey Drake. Finally in the Spent Gnat stage, generally in the late afternoon or evening, the Grey Drake, after dropping its eggs, falls with outspread wings exhausted on the water, and is eagerly taken by the fish.

There is a bewildering variety of artificial May-fly patterns, winged and hackled, wet and dry, from which the angler may make his choice, yet experience strongly inclines one to the belief that, when the May-fly is on the fish are by no means so fastidious about shape and colouring as at other times. I do not go so far as to say that any fly you throw them is the fly they want, but I am satisfied that they display a catholicity of taste which is certainly not one of their normal attributes. I call to mind an occasion when I arrived on the bank of a river I was to fish to find myself, most unexpectedly, in the midst of a big May-fly rise, and I had not a May-fly with me. The nearest approach my fly-case contained was a big March Brown, so I put that on my cast, and killed over 20 trout. This may be an extreme case, but it is a fact.

H. T. Sheringham appears to have had very little faith in the "exact imitation" theory as applied to May-flies, for he wrote: "I have no great belief in the superiority of one pattern of body over another. . . . It is partly the expense of winged flies that has made me take to hackle May-flies of the kind known as 'straddle-bugs'. But it is partly that I have found them to all intents and purposes as effective." And the Straddle-bug possesses so little claim to "exact imitation" that opinion is divided as to whether it was originally intended to imitate the immature nymph or the physical wreck of the mature insect.

The artificial May-fly is fished wet or dry, upstream or across-and-down, by the methods described in the last two preceding chapters. At the commencement of the hatch, before the trout have started surface feeding, the wet fly, Straddle-bug or other hackled pattern will usually be found to be most productive of sport. During the next phase, when the Green Drake is on the water, the floating fly is likely to do most execution. Many of the winged patterns are most artistically dressed, marvels of skill and dainty attractiveness, yet I very much doubt if they hold any advantage over the hackled form. Anyhow, if you use the winged fly, I strongly advise you to take Sheringham's tip and oil only the hackles, and *not* the wings.

When the Spent Gnat is falling the Straddle-bug, fished dry, will often prove a good killer, although there are patterns which are closer imitations of the natural insect.

If during a rise of the May-fly the fish will not take the artificial fished upstream and dry, try it wet, across-and-down, or try it upstream and sunk. There are occasions when they will take it in one way and not another.

Useful dressings of the May-fly, wet, dry and nymph, will be found in Chapter XXIV.

CHAPTER X

NYMPH FISHING

A PHILOSOPHIC poet once wrote:

> How sad it is to sit and pine
> The long half-hour before we dine!

but how much sadder must it have been for the old-time dry-fly man of the chalk streams, galled with the yoke of stern Purist dogma, to sit and pine the long half-hour—or, maybe, the long half-day—before the trout visibly commenced to dine? His angling hours were mainly spent in waiting, waiting, waiting for the rise with the same sort of long-suffering that inspired the Governor of North Carolina's historic utterance to the Governor of South Carolina, "It's a long time between drinks".

But the reign of asceticism could not last unchallenged for ever. There arose in the ranks a rebel, yclept Skues—G. E. M. of that ilk—an evangelist of common sense, an iconoclast, a breaker of Purist images, who bore before astonished eyes a banner with a strange device, "Minor Tactics of the Chalk Stream".

Patiently, perseveringly and convincingly Skues sought to teach the dry-fly man that, with the adoption of a wider tolerance, without sacrificing the true element of sportsmanship, and still retaining in his practice, with a little modification, those tenets of dry-fly fishing that really mattered, he could, in the absence of a rise, by fishing a suitable fly under water instead of on the surface, dispel to a great extent the weary hours of waiting, and add to chalk-stream joys a new fascination unsurpassed, if not unequalled, by fishing the floater.

Gradually Skues's new doctrine took root, and grew, until to-day, under the name and style of "Nymph Fishing", *vice* "Minor Tactics of the Chalk Stream", it has attained to the status of modern orthodoxy and is in common practice on our dry-fly waters as a highly skilled branch of angling closely allied to dry-fly fishing proper.

In certain respects nymph fishing closely resembles upstream wet-fly fishing on the moorland rivers, as already described: the chief differences being adaptations of method to suit the more slowly-running waters and the chalk-stream angler's better opportunities for spotting a particular fish and casting to it, instead of searching the water for any fish that haply may be encountered.

The first aim, then, of the chalk stream nymph fisher is to detect a fish feeding under water. Perhaps it is exclusively interested in the nymphs as they rise from the depths for their metamorphosis into the winged fly on the surface, in which case its grab at the insect may, without breaking the surface, produce a watery hump or bulge. Hence we have come to refer to trout producing this manifestation as "bulging" fish. Again, in shallow water the tip of a waving tail often indicates that its possessor is, standing almost on its head, busily engaged in fossicking on the bottom for shrimps, caddis grubs or other low-lying larvæ. And, still again, if the direction of the light is right, the eye may detect in the limpid water, perhaps over a gravel patch or perhaps above a bed of weeds, an alert snapper-up of unconsidered trifles in the shape of wandering shrimps, nymphs borne within its ken by the current, or those free-swimming nymphs possessing the larval capability of voluntary subaqueous movement from one spot to another. Now it is seen darting to the right, now to the left, now advancing, now with a quick right-about chasing an elusive morsel that has given it the slip, but always returning to its former position. While occupied in any of these nutritive functions the trout is fair game for the nymph fisher.

Only one fly is mounted on the cast, and the tackle is that employed in dry-fly fishing, so that, should circumstances render it advisable, a change can at once be made from nymph to dry fly and vice versa. The reel line is greased to make it float, and the fly is left ungreased to allow it to sink. To this end the fly is dressed with absorbent materials, including hen hackles. Some nymph fishers grease the cast except the last foot or so, the reason they adduce being that, with the upper part of the cast afloat, they can better detect that slight stoppage of the line which is often the only indication that the fish has taken the fly, and this momentary hesitation is much more difficult to spot on the slow-moving chalk stream than on the rapid river. Others do not find greasing the cast any great advantage, and there is always the danger of the grease getting onto that part of the line next to the fly whose special mission is to sink as rapidly as possible.

Unless the fly sinks quickly it may well be that it passes futilely over the feeding fish without coming within its notice. It *must* commence to sink the moment it enters the water, and therein lies a difficulty, for a few false casts through the air to get out the correct length is often sufficient to impart to it a fatal amount of momentary buoyancy. To obviate this various dodges are resorted to. One man, after he has got out his length, allows his fly to trail in the stream below him until it is well sodden before making his cast. Another applies a liberal dose of saliva to the fly and the last foot of gut. A third treats fly and last link of gut with wet mud; while a fourth anoints them with glycerine. One's thoughts naturally turn to lead as a possible and permanent solution of the difficulty, but so far it has not proved an unqualified success. In most instances the wrapping of the lead strip under the body dressing makes it too bulky for a good imitation of the natural nymph.

The stoppage of the line is not the only indication of a subaqueous rise. Often in the smooth clear water of the dry-fly river the flash of the taking fish as it turns is visible to the observant eye—the twinkling flash of which Skues sings in his merry lilt, "Little Brown Wink", in *The Way of a Trout with a Fly*. I quote a couple of verses:

> Oh, thrilling the rise at the lure that is dry,
> When the slow trout comes up to the slaughter,
>> Yet rather would I
>> Have the turn at my fly,
> The cunning brown wink under water.
>> That cute little wink under water!
>> Mysterious wink under water!
>>> Delightful to ply
>>> The subaqueous fly,
>> And watch for the wink under water.
>
> I care for no trout that comes up with a splash
> To capture the fly that I've brought her;
>> Let the trout that will dash
>> At my fly with a flash,
> But tip me the wink under water.
>> The gleaming brown wink under water,
>> The golden-brown wink under water,
>>> When I think I descry
>>> The quick turn at my fly,
>> The fleeting brown wink under water.

In nymph fishing the avoidance of drag is not nearly so important as in fishing the floating fly, as the trout are habituated to the sight of free-swimming nymphs voyaging more or less across the current instead of moving willy-nilly with it on the surface after reaching the dun stage.

Those who are firm believers in the "exact imitation" theory as applied to nymph fishing are often hard put to it to determine what particular insect the fly they put on should imitate. Should there be on the water a few duns which have escaped the hungry jaws of the enemy as they rose to the surface, and he can secure one of these for identification, it is reasonably safe to assume that the fish are feeding on the nymphs of that species; but if there be no tangible clue for his guidance, the best he can do is to mount the imitation of what he thinks they are most likely to be taking under the prevailing circumstances.

In the close imitation class of nymphs Skues gives in *The Way of a Trout with a Fly* the following dressing of the Iron Blue Dun:

Hook.—No. oo round bend.
Body.—Mole's fur on crimson tying silk, well waxed, the silk exposed for the two or three turns at the tail end.
Whisks.—Two or three strands of soft, mobile, white hackle, quite short.
Legs.—The very short, nearly black, hackle from the throat of a cock jackdaw, not exceeding two turns.

The next two patterns are given me by "G. E. M. S." as a brace of his most efficient nymph dressings:

Variant of the Pale Watery Dun

Hook.—No. 15, Down-eyed Pennell Sneck.

Tying silk.—Abdomen, cream, waxed with colourless wax ; thorax, hot orange.

Hackle.—Reddish centre with white points, short, not over two turns.

Whisks.—Pale guinea fowl neck (not white), two strands, short.

Rib.—Fine silver wire over abdomen only.

Body.—Cream coloured baby seal.

Thorax.—Ruddy rabbit's poll, dyed Red Ant or Red Spinner.

JULY DUN

Hook.—No. 15 or 16, Down-eyed Pennell Sneck.

Tying silk.—Ordinary orange.

Hackle.—Dark rusty hen, short, not over two turns.

Whisks.—Pale (not white) guinea fowl, two strands, short.

Rib.—Fine gold wire on abdomen.

Body.—Abdomen, pale fox cub dyed brightly in picric acid; thorax, dark blue fur of English squirrel or mole.

These patterns have been specially designed for the South Country chalk streams, and are not always suitable for use on other waters. The tackle dealers supply a galaxy of alleged imitations of well-known flies in their nymph stage—and a few fancies which represent no fly in creation—but it is quite a common practice to use in nymph fishing, popular patterns of wet flies dressed small, *i.e.* on hooks no larger than No. 0, except in the case of Greenwell's Glory, which I, personally, fancy on a No. 1. My own selection of wet flies for this style of fishing would be: Greenwell's Glory, Gold-ribbed Hare's Ear, Orange Partridge, Waterhen Bloa, Dark Watchet, Pheasant Tail, Tup's Indispensable, Half Stone, and Poult Bloa. These flies, when wet, with their soft hackles a-quiver in the current, certainly do bear some resemblance to the nymph. In the case of nymph fishing with a winged fly it is advisable to have the wings tied so that they have a pronounced backward slope.

To dress the flies specially as nymphs a rough-and-ready, but generally a successful, plan is to take the ordinary dressing for the wet fly, omit the wings, tie the body with a hump at the shoulder, confine the hackle to two turns left very short, and also leave the whisks short.

The ethics of nymph fishing provide ground for much debate on the chalk streams, where the rigid disciplinarians would bar everything but casting to the spotted feeder, and would regard all fancies as anathema —if they did not ban the nymph altogether. On the other hand, the latitudinarians would not hesitate to "prospect" for a feeding fish if one were not in evidence, and would accept the fancy as a very pleasant help in time of trouble. With that I leave it.

Nymph fishing on its original lines is confined to the slow-running rivers. Adapted as nearly as it can be— and that is a very long way from those original lines— to the rapid streams where the dry-fly technique is not applicable, it simply resolves itself into wet-fly fishing upstream with one fly, and "prospecting" at that. Thus, seeing that it is now generally held that the trout takes the wet fly of, say, the Yorkshire and Devonshire patterns, for the nymph, the wet-fly fisher, like the man who had been talking prose all his life and never knew it, may exalt himself in the discovery that, in a fashion, he has been nymph fishing all his life without being aware of the fact. But that is a thing quite apart from nymph fishing as it was originally designed and as it is understood on the chalk streams.

CHAPTER XI

LAKE FISHING

IT seems to be the general custom among writers on lake trout fishing to unburden themselves of a few sweeping observations betokening their disapproval of, if not disgust for, bait fishing on lochs, loughs, meres and reservoirs, and then devote themselves exclusively to fly fishing; or to ignore the use of baits and spinning lures entirely. And yet there are thousands of lake anglers who never fish anything but the bait; there are many lakes on which fly fishing is hopeless, and, as a general rule, it is only bait fishing that will account for the capture of the outsize cannibals. Look through the big fish lists, and note the preponderance of the double-figured specimens taken by trolling among those the method of whose capture is recorded. Although I personally prefer fly fishing, I deal here first with bait fishing as the most neglected—from the literary point of view—branch of the subject of this chapter.

Trolling, as it is now understood, is the most popular form of spinning on the great lakes of Scotland and Ireland. It is practised from a boat, and here, let me say, the most important item in the troller's outfit— and the same applies to fly fishing—is a boatman who knows his job. There is nothing much more irritating than the excitable gillie who loses his head at a critical juncture. I was once spinning for loch trout and had hooked a good fish that, after the first wild rush, flashed up a yard into the air, glittering in the sunshine in all the splendour of bronze and silver splotched with crimson.

"A 5-pounder if he's an ounce!" yelled the boatman, and the estimate was passed unanimously. So far, so good; but at the sight of the fish the boatman's wits scattered to the four winds of Heaven, and he was deaf to all remonstrance, as he shipped his oars and grabbed the landing-net although the battle was only just beginning. Instead of keeping me on sporting terms with my fish, he let the boat drift at the will of a snoring breeze, so that I was, as it were, playing both boat and fish at the same time. I did my best—so did the fish—but I could not avert disaster against such heavy odds, and eventually, after a prolonged fight, the fish came unstuck. The boatman's jaw dropped in speechless mortification, and, to the best of my recollection, I said, "Dear me!" With an efficient boatman I should have had that fish long before it got off.

The competent boatman should know the best fishing grounds under the prevailing conditions and the most likely depths at which to fish. Once a fish is hooked, he should, without being prompted, manœuvre his craft so as to afford all the assistance possible to the rodster. Seated in the stern, it is usual for the angler to have a couple of rods out, projecting outboard from opposite sides of the boat and kept in place by thole-pins, with the baits spinning 30, 40 or even 50 yds. in the wake, and weighted so that the two lures are fishing at different depths. The baits may be either natural or artificial, the former for choice, and in that case may take the shape of large minnows, gudgeon or, at a pinch, any small fish that may be available. On some of the Irish loughs an "eel-tail" is a favourite bait. Not only is the eel-tail an attractive lure, but it wears well and, having been prepared in any odd spell of leisure, may be preserved in salt for use at any time. And this is the manner of its preparation: For lake fishing take a medium-sized eel, and skin it down to a point about 3 in. from the tip of the tail. Cut off the

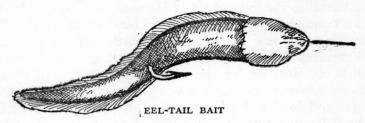

EEL-TAIL BAIT

flesh and backbone at the point down to which you have skinned, and here insert in the remaining flesh the point of a large hook, whipped on stout salmon gut, and bring it out an inch or so nearer the tip oɪ the tail. The troll may be weighted with a large shot on the gut immediately above the shank of the hook, or a strip of lead may be wound round the shank itself. It then remains to gather the loose skin round the end of the shank, lead included, and tie securely with waxed thread or silk, after which turn back the skin, like a stocking "turn-over", over the tie, trim off to a depth of $\frac{1}{2}$ in., and sew the edge to the tail.

The size of the bait and the strength of the tackle should be in accordance with the size of the fish likely to be encountered. Thus, in a lake holding pike it is often advisable to use a fine wire trace. Of artificial baits I prefer phantoms of various colours—brown and gold, blue and silver, or painted to imitate a gudgeon. Devons and spoons are also used with effect.

Seated in the stern, the troller draws down a loop of line on each rod and places on it, on the bottom of the boat, a small flat stone, the jumping up of which is the signal that a fish has taken the bait and the battle is joined.

As I have said, the competent boatman knows the likeliest localities; generalising, it is worth while to follow Horace's advice and,

> Not always tempt the distant deep,
> Nor always timorously creep
> Along the treacherous shore.

In other words, good trolling ground is often found where the gently shelving bed of the inshore water more or less suddenly dips to a deeper level. The boat is rowed steadily—*not* quickly—and on some waters the out-board motor has taken the place of oars, in which case care should be taken to regulate the speed to the requirements of the occasion.

The hardest thing about a day's trolling is the boat seat. If sport is brisk this is not so noticeable; but during a long spell of hope deferred the stern, unyielding after thwart of a boat may become too, too reminiscent of the cushionless pew of an Auld Licht kirk during a two hours' sermon. The remedy is a sponge-rubber cushion.

But trolling is not the only possible method of spinning from a boat. Personally I have found enjoyable sport, where the water was not too deep, in casting the minnow on light tackle, as in river fishing, from a fixed-spool reel while the craft was allowed to drift slowly stern first. At the worst it keeps you occupied. Seated on the after thwart, a flick of the rod sends your bait flying 30 yds. to your left, to be spun home, when a backhand flick flings it 30 yds. to your right, and by the time you have recovered it the boat has drifted just far enough to provide for your next cast to the left to cover fresh water. And so, alternately throwing to left and right, you pursue the even tenor of your way until the preliminary tug foretokens the coming tussle.

Spinning from the shore is, of course, possible, but, obviously, the area of water that can be commanded by the shore fisher is very limited. He has to make the best of what he can reach. Still, sensational results may be his, as witness the experience of J. H. R. Bazley in Blagdon's early days, his account of which—he was fishing from the shore—in his *Fun with the Fishing Rod* concludes with: "The tension over and the fish landed —it must have taken fully forty minutes to kill him— my hands trembled so violently that I could scarcely remove the flight. They had been watching the fight through binoculars at the inspection house, where a warm welcome awaited me, for mine—5 lb., 6¼ lb. and 8¼ lb.; total 19½ lb.—were the only fish caught."

Working from the shore, both in spinning and fly fishing, waders will be found a great advantage, as with their aid much more water may be covered.

Live-baiting is very occasionally indulged in in lake fishing, a small fish being mounted on snap tackle or in the manner described in the chapter on "Thames Trouting". In *Angling for Game Fish* John Bickerdyke briefly describes a method of live-baiting of which I have no personal knowledge. He says: "On some Irish lakes a live fish—usually a small trout—is hooked through both lips, and *very slowly* drawn after a boat, at the end of 50 yds. of line. The pull of the boat prevents the bait getting to the bottom. Some very large trout are caught in this way."

The worm accounts for more lake trout than one would gather from the perusal of polite angling litera- ture, the worm fisher's golden opportunity arriving when the swollen tributaries pour their alimentary delicacies into the lake, and the trout, with an eye ever open to the main chance, gather to the banquet. The bait, mounted on single hook or Pennell tackle, and shotted, is cast out into the area where the violence of the spate is rapidly losing itself in the greater waters, allowed to sink, moved a little after a pause, and so the likely spots are searched. Another method of worm fishing in vogue on some of the Scottish lochs is practised at night from rocky points commanding deeper water. The procedure is simple; the bait is cast out and allowed to sink to the bottom and wait there until a foraging trout comes along and appropriates it.

A form of bait fishing very popular on the Irish loughs, dapping with the natural fly, is described in a later chapter.

Fly fishing, the highest form of lake angling, bristles with problems of the why-and-wherefore order that have long intrigued the delver into piscatorial mysteries and about which the majority of anglers do not bother their heads. The latter are concerned, first, last and all the time, with the methods employed in catching trout, and it is the purpose of this volume to serve them.

By far the easiest and most effective way to fly-fish a lake is from a boat, and, on the score of economy, it is not unusual for two anglers to fish from the same craft. This, one stationed in the bows and the other in the stern, they may do with reasonable comfort, but three is a crowd which should be avoided at all costs. The boatman sits amidships, with one oar out on the windward side to ensure that the craft drifts broadside on down the breeze. A gentle wind will provide all the progress needed; but should the breeze prove too powerful, a stone slung over the windward side amidships and towed will reduce the speed of the drift.

The feeding ground of the trout interested in surface food is confined to the shallows, and to fish the fly on water over 10 or 12 ft. deep is a waste of time and energy. Should natural flies be hatching out, they will be blown towards the lee shore, and the probability is that the best sport will then be found in that direction, for, as pigs follow the pail, so will the trout temporarily change their quarters in accordance with Nature's shifting larder. Also, a fall in the water of the lake necessarily compels, and a rise invites, a residential change for the time being. Generally, however, the fish seem to keep to their recognised hunting grounds, such areas being selected on account of their permanent, if variable as to quantity, supply of bottom food on which the trout mainly subsist.

The chief food of the lake trout—other than the cannibals—consists of shrimps, snails, larvæ and such-like small beer, and these are found in greatest abundance on sandy shallows, in weed-covered shallow bays, in close proximity to the reed-beds, off gravelly spits, at the mouths of tributary streams, in the vicinity of upstanding rocks and under overhanging tree-fringed banks, all of which spots should carefully be searched with the fly.

There is a growing diversity of opinion as to the best length of rod for lake fly fishing. The old-timers were, almost to a man, wedded to the use of the double-handed weapon of 13 or 14 ft. in length. The modern movement is in favour of shorter rods generally, but the longer weapon—12 ft. is a good length—still has advantages. In fishing from the shore far more water can be covered, and in boat fishing the bob fly—to be referred to later—can be worked much more effectively.

It is argued that casting with a light 9- or 10-footer must be less tiring than with the 12-footer. On the other hand it is claimed that casting with the longer double-handed rod, its action balanced by a suitably heavy reel, is less fatiguing, seeing that the work is shared by both hands, whereas in the case of the shorter rod the whole of the burden is thrown upon one. There is the alternative of the single-handed 12-footer, but this, except in the hand of a powerful man, makes a toil of a pleasure. With this I leave the choice to the taste and fancy of the individual.

Thirty-five yards of dressed reel line, with the same length of backing, will be found sufficient, and there is no call for the reel line to be tapered. The reel line should not be too heavy. The gut cast for wet-fly fishing is not usually tapered, and may be 1X, 2X or 3X according to the conditions. It is customary to fish with three flies on the cast, in which case the cast should be 3 yds. in length, with 1 yd. separating the tail fly from the first dropper, and another 1 yd. between the first and second droppers. When a team of four flies is fished the cast should be lengthened to 4 yds., the flies being arranged the same distance apart as in the former instance.

The top dropper is called the " bob " fly, and its mission on the water is to dance lightly on the surface, in obedience to the rod, as the cast is drawn home, while the rest of the flies are fishing submerged. The more easily to effect this, the connecting link between the bob and the main cast should not be less than 4 in., while half that length of link is sufficient for the other droppers. It often happens that the bob fly proves the most fatal attraction.

But all this time our boat has been drifting with the breeze, our anglers casting down the wind in advance of the craft, or down and across, and drawing back the line steadily, or, perhaps, in three or four alternating draws and pauses, before making a fresh cast. Always the raising of the point of the rod should be regulated to keep the bob fly dancing seductively on the wavelets during as much of the recovery as possible.

Obviously, with two reckless casters in the boat, not only would there be constant danger of the lines fouling one another, but the boatman would be in imminent peril of being hooked in the back casts. Therefore, it behoves the man with the boatman on his right to confine himself to casting over his left shoulder, while the man with the boatman on his left casts only over his right shoulder. This may give the latter the advantage, so, to equalise matters, the two change positions, or the boat is turned round, at reasonable intervals.

Now, fishing in the manner I have described with the drifting boat, a great deal of water can be covered, but over some of the most likely spots the boat cannot be drifted, and this is where the one-man-in-a-boat scores, for the boatman can put him within casting distance of almost any desirable feeding area. And here let me say that, in addition to the likeliest places already mentioned, a patch or streak of foam should never be overlooked. These are carefully investigated from below by the trout on the chance of finding dainty insect morsels entangled therein, and a team of flies drawn through them will frequently add to the basket.

In fishing from the shore the cast and recovery are made in the same way as from a boat; the angler's chief problem is determining the best positions from which to operate, an important factor being the direction of the wind. It is a waste of time to fish dead water in the lee of a promontory, and if he can find a part of the shore where the breeze blows parallel with the coastline he should make the most of that. Such a section is easy to fish and usually productive of results.

Working along the edge of the water, he casts down the wind and slightly across, so that his flies fall 5 to 10 yds. to "seaward", whence they can be drawn home along the trough of the wavelets or, at any rate, obliquely across them. With an off-shore wind a longer line may be cast, and drawn back across the ripples, while with an on-shore breeze the fish are apt to lie closer in, and as the greater commotion in the water does much to conceal the angler from view, a short line be can used, and the cast should be made across the wind. This entails, of course, more exertion, but it is often well repaid.

In the river the trout takes up its position head up-stream, and waits for the current to bring its food to it, with the consequence that when there is a marked rise of a certain fly the fish devotes its attention exclusively to that article of diet and a subsequent autopsy reveals a homogeneous mass. In the lake there is no accom-modating current, and there is, in many instances, no rise worth mentioning. As a result the lake trout has to hunt for its food, scrounging what it can find, and a post-mortem examination of its alimentary system brings to light something in the nature of a "hetero-geneous conglomeration of incongruities". It follows, then, that the lake trout, through heredity or habit or both, is possessed of a more catholic taste than its brother of the stream, and will take patterns of artificials which bear no recognisable resemblance to any known living creature. Possibly the trout may take them for larvæ, beetles, or some tiny fish of no particular species; my own belief is that they take them because they appear to be alive and look like something good to eat.

The accumulated experience of generations of anglers seems to have established that the loch trout have a partiality for certain colours, and so many standard "lake flies" have been evolved, and these, along with a selection of river flies, usually dressed on a larger scale, form the regular ammunition of the wet-fly fisher. The following is a list of the most popular lake flies: Peter Ross, Greenwell's Glory, Butcher, Bloody Butcher, Dunkeld, Zulu, Grouse and Claret, Grouse and Green, Teal and Green, Woodcock and Yellow, March Brown, Blue Dun, Blae and Black, Red Palmer, Coch-y-bonddu, Alexandra, and Wickham's Fancy.

It is as well to have the patterns tied on two sizes of hooks, say Nos. 9 and 11 Redditch scale, or 6 and 4 New scale.

While wet-fly fishing is the general custom on the lakes, there seems to be a growing disposition in some quarters to employ the dry fly when and where the conditions are appropriate to the use of the floater. As, however, the visible rise of fish to the natural insect upon the surface of the water is essential to the successful employment of the dry fly, and such rises are, comparatively, infrequent; and, moreover, seeing that rough water, accompanied by a high wind, promptly drowns the fly and, in fishing from a quickly drifting boat, causes the fatal drag; the opportunities of the dry-fly man are very restricted. Any angler foolish enough to confine himself solely to dry-fly work on the lake would find himself for the greater part of his time—sometimes for days at a stretch—numbered among the unemployed. While the rise is on he may have, and often enough has, excellent sport, but at other times he must depend upon the wet fly. There is little opportunity for the Purist on the lake.

The same line will serve for both wet and dry fly, but, used with the latter, it must, of course, be greased, and the fly must be duly anointed in the manner described for river fishing. The ordinary dry-fly rod will serve, and it is much easier to fish the floater from the shore, or while wading, than from a boat. It is only the shallow waters, on or in whose bed the Ephemerids pass their larval existence, that are of interest to the dry-fly man. For this reason the shallow lakes, such as Loch Leven, will provide him with his best opportunities.

On the lakes there is much more of the chuck-and-chance element in dry-fly fishing than on the chalk streams. On the latter a feeding trout will rise in the same spot time after time; on the former you can never count on such a phenomenon. Owing to the fish's habit of snatching its meals in "promenade" fashion, the visible signs of two successive rises may be 2 or 3 yards apart, and it is uncertain where the fish will be by the time your fly alights on the water. You, therefore, cast to the spot where you think it is likely to be, and if the little tempter falls within eyeshot of the rover, it may, instead of gently sucking it under, come at it with a rush. If nothing happens you permit the fly to float for a couple of minutes or so, dry it with a few vigorous false casts, or even administer the amadou's absorbent aid, and try again at a fresh spot in the vicinity of the spreading rings.

As the lake trout does not feed so regularly on the imagines as does the chalk stream epicure, it is natural to suppose that, less familiar with the perfect insect, it is not nearly so critical in its tastes. Consequently the dry-fly fisher need not trouble himself to carry such a wide range of artificials. He will probably find a Greenwell's Glory the most serviceable pattern, as the most prevalent flies on the water are the Olives, and the Greenwell kills well when the Darker Olives are in evidence. A Pale Olive will serve when the lighter shades are hatching out, and a winged Iron Blue or a Dark Watchett will be wanted when the Iron Blues are abroad. The Blae and Black is another useful pattern.

Dressings of the flies mentioned in the foregoing will be found in Chapter XXIV.

CHAPTER XII

BUSTARD FISHING

THERE is a form of night angling for trout with the artificial fly, practised on the North of England and Border rivers, and especially on the Eden, known as Bustard fishing. It was anathema to the old Purist, and to-day is occasionally denounced as unsportsmanlike by fly-fishers of the higher cult who have never tried it.

In the matter of sporting ethics, however, there is little or nothing to choose between the Bustard fishing of the North Country wet-fly angler and the evening Sedge fishing of the South Country dry-fly man. The latter form of sport no less an authority than F. M. Halford admits within the scope of his work on *Dry-fly Fishing in Theory and Practice*. He says, writing of summer evening fishing, that after the angler is unable to see his own fly, the sport "may be slightly prolonged by fishing a big sedge and putting it on the water rather heavily. . . . As to evening fishing, it is distinctly good, and the night fishing, if I can call the period just after dusk so, even better. . . . Fine gut is quite unnecessary; in fact, coarse gut works better with large flies, and evidently there is no advantage in handicapping yourself when it is nearly dark . . . the fisherman being invisible until the fish is almost tired out and practically in the net." These observations, aimed at dry-fly angling, hit the very bull's-eye of North Country Bustard fishing; for on the northern streams there is no absolute darkness during the clear nights of summer, when the latter style is practised; and the cream of the sport is usually skimmed in that stage of semi-obscurity which follows dusk, say from ten o'clock to an hour or two after midnight. Indeed, so closely akin are the two styles of fishing that Major J. W. Hills, in *My Sporting Life*, says, "The bustard corresponds to the sedge of the Test", and Leonard West, in *The Natural Trout Fly and its Imitation*, states, "The largest species of Sedge (*Phryganea grandis*) is the Bustard of the north".

West is wrong, both lexicologically and entomologically; for "bustard"—no connection with the bird of that name—is a local North Country term for the big nocturnal moths, especially the Ghost moths and others of the *Hepialidæ* (in other North Country districts they are known as "buzzards") which in the height of summer may be seen flitting over the meadows in the gloaming; and, while the imitation of the big Sedge will take trout in night fishing, the old standard dressings of the Bustard are, obviously, intended to represent the moths.

Let me try to give an impression of this rather weird form of trout fishing as it is actually pursued. Snatching an early supper, we slip down to the riverside in the first soft shadow of twilight on a typical July or August evening, for a few hours of sport while the rural workaday world is comfortably snoring.

Although the sun has been down behind the hill for an hour or more, it is still too light for the Bustard; but half a mile of alternating dancing stream and glassy glide intervene between us and the scene we have spotted for our later operations, and as we make our way upstream we succeed in landing two or three decent fish on the Governor and the Coachman, dressed on No. 3 hooks.

The dusk is rapidly overtaking us, quickly to deepen into the nearest approach to darkness of which the summer night is capable, as we arrive at the length we have selected—a long reach, half gliding flat, half pool shelving off into wide gravelly shallows, for the old cannibalistic patriarchs, harmful in the river as pike of their inches, come forth from their holts under cover of darkness to seek what they may devour on the shallows. The ideal Bustard fishing water is free from snags and other obstructions, with no tree nor bush to interfere with the back cast of the line, and edged with closely cropped grass banks and gently sloping beaches of pebbles, so that the fish may, if small, be lifted clean from the water or, if too heavy for that treatment, run ashore. A landing-net is a nuisance on account of the hooks catching in the meshes.

With the aid of a pocket torch a Bustard is knotted on to the end of the 2-yds. cast of stout undrawn gut, a second being mounted 1 yd. above the first, dropper-wise, and the pair launched out into the unseen on their voyage of luck, for Bustard fishing is truly a sport of the "chuck-and-chance-it" type. The cast is made across the stream and the flies allowed to swim down until they hang in the current below, or they may be worked gently with a sink-and-draw motion.

There are natural trout flies which persistently defy the skill of the ambitious fly-dresser earnestly aiming at that artificial perfection only attained by the optician who advertised "glass eyes so absolutely true to nature that even the wearers themselves cannot see through the deception". But no such difficulty faces the fly-tier in producing an effective, if somewhat crude, imitation of the big brown, yellow, or white night moth. Many patterns and variations in colour and material are employed in dressing the Bustards. Major Hills refers to the "traditional" Bustard as one "winged with swan, either white or dyed red or yellow, with a silk body to match, edged with peacock herl". A clerical friend of mine tried the experiment of dressing one with yellow mohair body, simply hackled with a red feather which the domestic parrot had shed. He found it so successful that the parrot, possibly with a little assistance in the moulting process, lent itself to the sport for many seasons.

However, the majority of old Bustard fishers pin their faith, and occasionally their trout, to three general patterns—the brown, the white, and the yellow—which may be dressed thus: BROWN—body, light tawny brown chenille; wings, feather from the wing of a brown owl; hackle, buff; tail, a tag of white kid. WHITE—body, white chenille; wings, a white feather from a white pigeon; hackle, light buff; tail, a tag of white kid. YELLOW—body, yellow chenille ribbed with red silk; wings, a cream feather; hackle, buff; tail, a tag of white kid. In all these patterns mohair may be substituted for chenille, and in the case of the yellow Bustard, instead of wings and hackle as above, a light yellow hackle is sometimes used struck, palmer-fashion, from head to tail. The hooks used may be No. 5.

To the tyro the situation is saturated with the witchery of unaccustomed night. The crooning breeze sighs eerily through the woods that loom vaguely across the river; the water laps gently at our feet. Now and then, with startling abruptness the *plop*! of a feeding fish flings itself athwart the senses; wood owls *hoo-hoo* across the dale. Sometimes unseen wings whirr and whistle overhead; the shrill squeal of a hare strikes sharply from a nearby hedgerow; once an unsuspected cow coughs—coughs suddenly and vigorously—close to our shoulder, and the awful sound for a moment sets us a-tremble in every limb.

There is a fearsome fascination in the sense of loneliness among the outdoor voices of the night. When, lying awake in the dark watches in one's bed, all the rest of the house asleep, how impressive is every little creak of a stair-board springing back to normality after the weight of the footstep on it hours before! Out in the open, under the midnight stars by the riverside woodlands, God's stairs creak unspeakably more impressively, while, wraith-like, a cold faint light hangs low above the northern fells, slowly creeping eastward towards the dawn of another day. Looking upstream, the surface of the water shines dimly with a ghostly glimmer; looking down, the pool is an inky flood of invisibility.

With a wave of the rod the line uncurls over the dark water; somewhere the huge flies drop, and drift along with the current, but we cannot see them. Moving a yard or two at each fresh throw, the line has been flung out three times, when the mystic signal comes along the extended cord, out of the unseen to the sensitive touch of the expectant hand, that something has come in contact with the hook. There is no direct evidence for the moment what that something is. It may be one of those irritating snags, which, out of pure cussedness, lie hidden all day in the depths and rise up in the darkness to foul the angler's tackle and inspire unholy thoughts; it may be the discarded salmon-tin or the derelict boot; again, it may be a trout, and we strike on suspicion. After that there is no longer any doubt on the point, as a reluctant $\frac{1}{2}$-pounder, lustily protesting all the way, is quickly hauled ashore, unhooked, despatched with a crack of the spine, and pocketed. In night fishing the reduction of the angler's impedimenta to a minimum adds greatly to his comfort, and by having a couple of large "poacher's pockets" in his jacket, lined with detachable mackintosh linings, the use of a creel is obviated.

Next a sharp tug is followed by no result beyond a sudden slackening of the line—the consequence, perhaps, of a prankish troutlet's runaway knock, and then the fun grows faster for half an hour, fish coming to bank at cheeringly frequent intervals, until one of the patriarchs is encountered. Bang he goes with a terrific rush, and in spite of our determination to give no law save on the direst compulsion, the reel screeches and a dozen yards of line whizz out into the unfathomable before we can get the buccaneering rascal sufficiently in hand to hustle him. A couple of minutes of palpitating blindfold tug-of-war ensues, and in the excitement of the duel in the dark all sense of loneliness vanishes. At first inch by inch, then less slowly, we reel up, never relaxing the strain for a moment, and with quickened pulse pounding the drums of victory, the vanquished patriarch is run ashore on the cobbles at our feet.

Compared with this incident the landing of the subsequent ½- and ¼-pounders yields only minor thrills; yet, with misses and catches, the uncanny sport goes on until, after the clock in the old church tower has clanked out the hour of one, the fish go off the feed, and we saunter contentedly homeward.

And so, as Mr Pepys would have said, to bed, but not before we have turned out in the larder eight brace of trout, averaging three to the pound, and have crowned the dish with the noble proportions of the patriarch, whose weight the kitchen scales have certified to be just an ounce under 2 lb.

Bustard fishing may not rank high in the scale of scientific angling, but it has a fascination of its own, and certainly possesses the merit of clearing out old-stagers which are useless to the fly fishers of ordinary methods and are better out of the river than in it.

The Bustard season commences in June, is at its best in July, and extends into August.

Some North Country anglers do not hesitate to wade while fishing the Bustard, selecting a broad flat of, practically, a uniform depth of 18 in. or so; and, working down the middle of the river, throwing alternately to left and right. There is, however, a certain amount of risk attached to wading at night, and the practice should never be adopted unless the wader be perfectly familiar with every yard of the bed of the stream, for at a single step he may find himself struggling in a deep hole.

I have heard the story told of an angler wading a Cumberland river while Bustard fishing in company with a local fisherman, whose earnest protestations that he knew every hole in the stream had induced the other to take the risk. Soon the stranger abruptly flopped overhead where the bed dropped at once from a foot to a fathom in depth, and only scrambled out again with difficulty.

"Confound you!" he roared at the local man, as soon as he recovered his speech. "Didn't you tell me you knew every hole in the river?"

"Yes, I do", imperturbably rejoined the local. "That's one of 'em."

CHAPTER XIII

THE FLY ROD AND THE MINNOW

BEFORE we consider fishing with the spinning minnow as a specialised branch of trout fishing, and before we hang up the fly rod on the rack, let us give a thought to how, in the hands of the all-round trout fisher on the moorland river, that fascinating implement may be, and is, used in conjunction with the minnow as an emergency measure when untoward conditions render the service for which it was originally intended stale, flat, and unprofitable.

The rapid river is a fickle creature, prone to sudden changes, and the majority of our trout fishers do not dwell in leisured ease on the banks of trout streams, ready to spring into action the moment the river assumes a condition favourable for the practice of their pet particular form of the sport. However much we may love to gush over the flowers that grow on the banks or drink in the liquid notes of the feathered choirs on the adjacent premises, the fundamental object of trout fishing is to catch trout; and to do this the average angler must be prepared to take the moorland river as he finds it and make the best of his luck, good or bad.

It is recorded that the cynic has said, "I understand that on the wet-fly river the fly rod is so called because, in the odd moments when it is not being used for clear-water worming, or Creeper fishing, or Stone-fly fishing, or bait fishing with maggots or other objectionable small reptiles, or dibbing with Bluebottles, or worming in a flood, or swimming the worm for grayling, it may, at a pinch, be pressed into service for casting a leash of artificial flies over the stream".

Well, hardly that, but a 10½-ft. split-cane fly rod, not too whippy, can be put to a variety of purposes as an understudy to a battery of special weapons.

August is notoriously the worst trout-fishing month of the season—at any rate, for the fly-fisher. In any summer of heat and drought the wet-fly rivers have run down to their lowest ebb, the once lively rapids are reduced to anæmic trickles, and the merry roar of the cascade has sunk to a hoarse whisper. There is no sign of a rise on the shimmering surface of the shrunken pools; for all evidence to the contrary the trout are indulging in a siesta that will, probably, be prolonged until, if such a thing should materialise, the evening rise. Even the upstream worm may fail to interest them—it often does in August, though why I cannot tell; they will usually take it readily enough in July.

This, then, is distinctly the angler's opportunity to display his skill in making the best of a bad job should he only have his fly rod available, and should he have taken the precaution to stow a handful of salted minnows in the corner of his creel. Of course, the best equipment for making the most of such an opportunity consists of a light casting rod and a fixed-spool reel— concerning which I shall have something to say later —but, in the absence of such, the angler, with his fly rod, may save the day from complete disaster.

It is to be presumed that if he should have had the forethought to furnish himself with minnows he will also have provided himself with what is now generally listed as an Aerial (its original name was "A R I E L"

—the inventor's initials, I believe) tackle and trace. This flight, which is, in my opinion, by far the most suitable for small minnows, is made up of a notched lead, intended to be thrust down the throat of the minnow, and this lead not only supplies all the weight that is needful, but gives rigidity to the upper part of the bait where it is wanted, and three treble hooks.

The triangles are whipped on two short lengths of gut, one on one length, two on the other tandem fashion, and these two pieces of gut pass through a hole in the lip of the lead, above which they are joined together. The two upper trebles are fixed in position by inserting one hook of each into a shoulder of the bait so that they arm opposite sides of the minnow. The tail is then caught up by the remaining treble in a curve suitable for producing an attractive spin.

AERIAL TACKLE

Commencing operations at the foot of a stream, the angler, having hitched his trace to his fly line and baited his tackle, draws off what length of line he can command—the longer the rod, the longer the spin—and casts upstream as he would in clear-water worm fishing. The whole width of the attenuated stream should be fished, but the edges are likely to yield the best returns. Here, then, he drops his bait as lightly as his skill will permit, and as the water is probably so thin as barely to cover a fish, he must immediately commence to work the bait by drawing it down towards himself with the rod point, otherwise he is likely to foul the gravel at the bottom.

And the working of the bait calls for the display of

his finest art, for, should he not draw it down quicker than the flow of the current, it will not spin, while, should he hurry it too much, he will have the irritating experience of seeing fish chasing it to within a yard or two of his feet, and then darting away before they have screwed up their courage to the grabbing point.

Wading is essential to successfully approaching the trout, and even then every movement should be made without splash and with as little disturbance of the water as possible. Every little eddy and every run between upstanding boulders should be searched, and as a trout firmly seizes the bait the strike is made and the somersaulting fish brought downstream to the landing-net.

There is another way in which the natural minnow can be used with the fly rod in fishing the deeper water, the deeper eddies, and the tree-fringed corners of pools. It is known as drop minnow fishing, and closely resembles, in a miniature form, trolling for pike with snap tackle. At one time a single hook with a leaded shank was the angler's only choice in tackle for this method of fishing, and that meant the employment of a baiting-needle and waiting for the trout to gorge the bait before striking. Now, however, both these objections are met by the use of an improved tackle provided with a long-tapered pear-shaped lead, furnished with an eyelet, at the thick end, to which the gut is attached. On the gut are whipped successively two trebles and a smaller hook, as shown in the illustration. The lead is thrust down the throat

DROP MINNOW
TACKLE

of the minnow, which is then turned back alongside the gut, the two triangles are fixed in place by inserting a hook of each in the side of the bait, and the single hook is passed through the tail of the minnow, the body of which is not curved as in the spinning bait.

The minnow is worked with a sink-and-draw motion —allowed to plumb the mysterious depths, which it often does in a zigzag course, and then jerked upward, to dive again. With the tackle described the strike can be made immediately the trout is felt to seize the bait. It is possible, but more difficult, to fish the drop minnow in the streams, but the slack water under overhanging banks and the deep eddies will be found the most productive of sport.

In writing of preserved minnows carried by the flyfisher I mentioned salted ones only, for the reason that I have found the trout prefer the salted article on the drop tackle before one treated with one or other of the various formalin prescriptions. It may be that they then have a better opportunity for a critical sniff than as the spinning bait flashes into their ken, and, anyhow, there is little doubt that they do like a salted minnow.

The drawback is that the salted minnow presents a dried-up mummified appearance, and is, consequently, a trifle more difficult to bait; but, on introduction to the water, it quickly plumps out to normal proportions. Moreover, the preparation of the salted minnows is a very simple matter. Kill the minnows by flicking them on the head with the finger-nail, and dab them dry with a soft cloth. Now spread on one half of a strip of calico a layer of common salt—*not* prepared (and adulterated) table salt—and lay the minnows on it in rows. Spread another layer of salt over them, fold over that the remaining portion of the calico, and roll up. The minnows thus pickled will last for weeks.

Here is still another way in which the fly rod is used for fishing the minnow—if the live article is available —and that is by live baiting with float tackle. Many North Country anglers use the little globular cork float with a wooden plug which is commonly associated with swimming the worm for grayling, others a small cork float with a quill plug. The gut should be reasonably fine, say 3X; indeed it is not unusual for the angler to improvise the tackle with the aid of his tapered fly cast. No. 9 (Redditch scale) is a convenient size for the hook, which may be passed through both lips of the bait, or, as some prefer it, through the skin of the back immediately under the dorsal fin. One large shot, or a couple of small ones, should be nipped on the gut a few inches above the bait, and the float adjusted so that the minnow swims in mid-water. Time should be allowed for the trout to get the bait well into its mouth before the strike is made.

Finally, there are various patterns of fancy lures which may be classed under the head of fly minnows, specially designed for use with the fly rod and to be cast as flies. Many a time, after wandering upstream to the limit of my inclination or permission, and having to retrace my steps to get home, I have put on one of these lures, say a Halcyon Spinner, and by spinning across the streams and rippling fords on my way downstream, have added appreciably to the weight of my basket.

Of course, such lures as the Halcyon Spinner and the Spinning Alexandra should never be used on water reserved for fly only. In spite of their feathered dressings they are *not* flies, and are probably taken by the trout for gorgeously apparelled small fish.

CHAPTER XIV

SPINNING FOR TROUT: BAITS AND TACKLE

LOST in the hoary mists of antiquity is the name of the man, one of the all-round trout fisher's best friends and one of the trout's worst enemies, who discovered that a bait drawn through the water in scintillating gyrations is at times an almost irresistible attraction to the trout. Certainly spinning with the minnow was in vogue in Walton's day, for he not only tells how the natural minnow was used in this way, but he describes an artificial minnow, fearfully and wonderfully made of cloth and embroidered with coloured silks and silver thread "by a handsome woman that had a fine hand".

I do not think that even the adoption of dry-fly fishing has been a greater advance in angling progress in modern times than has been the substitution of present-day spinning tackle and tactics for those of grandfatherdom. In 1853 "Ephemera", probably the leading authority of his time, wrote: "The spinning rod need never be more than twelve feet in length, and it should be rather stiff than pliant. . . . The line should be stout, and of platted silk, and it should be oiled or varnished. . . . Uncoil from the winch as much line as is wanted, allowing the coils to rest at your feet. Let the bait hang not more than a yard from the top of the rod, then, poising and bringing back the rod either to the right or left, propel the bait somewhat upwards and forwards; and its weight, and the momentum given to it, will carry out all the coiled line. As soon as the bait falls in the water, commence drawing it towards you by short pulls of the line either with the right or left hand, making the bait spin straightly towards you with moderate speed."

This objectionable method of casting from the coils on the ground remained in practice long after "Ephemera's" day and generation—objectionable because the line picked up twigs and invited entanglement, and also because it was half rod-and-line fishing and half hand-lining. There was another, and more difficult, method by which the angler, with a bit of legerdemain, recovered line in figure-of-eight style on his thumb and finger, and cast from that orderly accumulation.

But all that has now gone. Almost universally we cast direct from the reel; our lines are fine and, for the most part, undressed; our rods are short and lissom; indeed, the first remark one acquaintance made on handling one of my spinning rods—an 8½-ft. split-cane—was, "Why, I could cast a dry-fly line with this!"

The best spinning bait—at any rate for river fishing —is the natural minnow, freshly killed if possible, otherwise preserved. There is no necessity for lugging about a cumbersome bait-can. The handiest means of transport is the common 1½-pint whisky bottle. Pour in water up to two-thirds of its capacity, when it will accommodate any number up to a score of minnows. Carried in the creel, your motions will aerate the water sufficiently to keep the minnows lively. The bottle should be corked. When a bait is wanted, remove the cork, tilt the bottle, and let the water trickle through your fingers until a minnow comes along into your hand. Re-cork the bottle, and kill the minnow with a flick of the finger-nail before baiting. Keep the water in the bottle up to the two-thirds mark by replenishments from the river as required. This also keeps the contents of the bottle cool.

The method of salting minnows has already been described. Thirty years or more ago, when formalin became generally known as a preservative, it was found that by being kept immersed in a 5 per cent solution of formaldehyde minnows retained their natural appearance for very long periods, and it was thought that the millennium of bait preservation had dawned. The only drawback to the new system was that the trout strongly disapproved of the formalined baits, which they persistently refused to take.

Various attempts have been made with more or less success to get rid of the objectionable flavour, the best of which, probably, takes the shape of soaking the minnows in a strong solution of salt and water for at least twenty-four hours after they are taken out of the formalin. A variation in the method of preservation, strongly recommended by Alexander Wanless in his *Science of Spinning for Salmon and Trout*, yields very good results. In this case the minnows are killed by immersion in 1 pint of water to which has been added a tablespoonful of formalin, which is the commercial name for a 40 per cent solution of formaldehyde, and in this they are left until they are rigid and somewhat swollen, which will probably be in a couple of days. They are then washed in cold water, and placed in a shallow dish containing a syrup composed of one part of sugar to four parts of water. In this they are exposed to the air for a few days, during which time the taint disappears, when they may be finally bottled in a fresh dose of the syrup and kept in a dark, cool place until wanted.

For mounting the natural minnow I, personally, prefer the Aerial tackle described in the last chapter, with the use of which the spin of the bait is produced by the curve produced by catching up the tail with the hindmost triangle. If the angler experiences any difficulty in getting the right curve, his problem can easily be solved by substituting one of the many varieties of spinners stocked at all the tackle shops, in which the spin is produced by a pair of small metal fans at the head of the minnow. In some of these—the Archer, for instance—the bait is kept straight by a metal spike thrust down the throat of the minnow. There is still another variety of good spinning tackle, easy to bait, in which the spin is effected by the curve of the bait, but that curve is produced by thrusting a pliable metal spindle down the throat, after which it, and the minnow, can be bent to any curve desired. I bar those forms of spinning tackle in which the necessity for using a baiting needle wastes time.

Now in the ordinary course of events, after a trout has seized a minnow in a hearty business-like manner, that minnow presents such a mangled appearance that the angler has no option but to retire it from active service, and, if sport is pretty brisk, this may mean that speedy exhaustion of the supply of baits is threatened. To avoid such disaster A. Holden Illingworth, the inventor of the Illingworth reel, devised the Scarab, which has proved a boon and a blessing to thousands of economists. The Scarab is a transparent sheath, enclosing the minnow, and protecting it from the jaws of the trout, while, at the same time, it imparts to it a straight spin, thus eliminating the difficulty (to some) of setting the tail to the correct curve. Clothed with the Scarab, a minnow will outlast five or six of its fellows fished in the nude, and the protective covering in nowise lessens its attractiveness.

The loach makes a good natural spinning bait, and

where big fish are looked for, as in Thames trouting and lake fishing, larger baits, such as bleak, dace and gudgeons, are frequently employed.

Of artificial spinning baits there are endless varieties, which may, for the most part, be classed as Devons, Phantoms, Quills, Wagtails, and Spoons. The Devon, a tubular metal arrangement with fans, roughly fish shape and cast in a piece, is usually either gold or blue and silver in colour and burnished. The gut is carried through the body of the bait, and terminates in a triangle at the tail. The Devon is most fatal in coloured water. (It can also be made of wood or plastic.)

The Phantoms are made of many kinds of materials from silk to mother-of-pearl, and much more nearly resemble the actual fish than do the Devons, as they are painted in various colours to imitate in glorified measure the species they are supposed to represent. They are furnished with spinning fans, and are usually armed with a triangle at the tail and two flying triangles of different lengths.

The Wagtail is, perhaps, best described as a Phantom, constructed of flexible material such as rubber, and split up the sides. It, too, is furnished with fans and armed like the Phantom. By many anglers it is esteemed one of the best artificial baits in the trout fisher's repertory.

The Quill is a light artificial minnow, made from a transparent natural quill suitably painted, and armed and furnished like the Phantom. Being very light, it is often fished on fine tackle in low, clear water with the fly rod.

The Spoon, so called from its resemblance to a domestic utensil of that name which had lost its shank and handle, may be variously coloured, say copper on the convex side, silver on the concave, though many of the trout Spoons are silvered on both sides. The shape of the Spoon causes it to spin.

Now, why does the spinning bait prove so attractive to a fish when it is utterly unaccustomed to hunting natural subaqueous whirligigs in the course of earning its living? The most lucid explanation I have come across is that supplied by H. D. Turing in his *Trout Fishing*: "In nature fish have been given protective coloration. The back is usually dark so that it does not reflect light coming down from above, but the flanks are often silvery and this acts as a mirror and enables the fish to become merged in its surroundings when it is on an even keel. If, however, a fish turns slightly in taking a fly or makes a quick movement while escaping to a bed of weed, for example, its flanks catch the light as it turns and advertise its whereabouts to any other fish in its vicinity. It is this 'flash' of the turn or wriggling movement which 'fish of prey' are accustomed to look for when on the feed, and it is this also which the spinning bait imitates."

As I have indicated, the era of the long spinning rod is past. At the present day there seems a tendency in some quarters to go to the opposite extreme, and rods of no more than five or six feet are advocated. These very short rods are effective under certain conditions, such as fishing from a boat, and when the overhead cast can be used; but they are likely to prove irritating handicaps under other conditions, such as fishing from the bank or when it is desirable to employ the popular side-swing cast. Personally I strongly favour a rod of 8 feet or even a few inches over that length. Such a length will serve well for bank fishing, wading, or boat fishing.

Perhaps I can best give some idea of the action of the modern spinning rod by asking you to take—in imagination, if you like—a 10½-ft. medium-actioned fly rod, *i.e.* one that is not pronouncedly too whippy nor too stiff, amputate 18 in. of the thin end of the top and 6 in. of the thick end of the butt; and what you have left will give you a rod which makes spinning with a 3-dr. bait and a fixed-spool reel a pleasure.

If, however, your fancy inclines you to the use of heavier baits and a revolving reel, then the action of the rod should be stiffened accordingly, but its length need not be increased. To get the best out of it the spinning rod should be of split-cane or tubular steel, and in either case should be fitted with agate rings.

For use with revolving reels of the Nottingham type a *reasonably* fine, undressed, braided silk line will be found the best, *i.e.* a line reasonably fine when compared with the gossamer threads used with a fixed-spool reel. A line with a breaking strain of 5 lb. would be a fine line for a Nottingham reel, while for the fixed-spool reel there is, for instance, a line made, of undressed silk, specially for the Illingworth reel in four thicknesses—1X, 2X, 3X, and 4X. The 4X is about the thickness of 60's sewing cotton, yet, for that thickness, is enormously strong, having a breaking strain of $1\frac{1}{2}$ lb., and is capable of dealing at a pinch, as I have found it, fairly comfortably with trout up to 5 lb. and 6 lb. Indeed, much heavier fish have been landed on it, but in such instances it has usually been a case of a good game played slowly.

Many devotees of the fixed-spool reel have, largely on the score of economy, gone in for fine gut-substitute lines in place of silk. Certainly gut substitute is much cheaper than silk, but it has an irritating objection to lying snugly on the spool until it is thoroughly soaked; dry, if not under restraint, it springs off the reel in coils in mutinous manner. A good soaking in warm water renders it meekly submissive, and in the intervals between its spells of active service it may be kept damp for quite a long while by the application, on the spool, to it of a rubber bandage. The main advantages claimed for the gut substitute are that it lasts much longer than silk, it does not kink so readily, and it is less visible to the fish.[1]

The spinning tackle is attached to the reel line through the medium of a length of gut called the trace. In spinning with the revolving reel in the ordinary way the trace may be from 1 yd. to 1½ yds. in length, with a loop at each end. The loop at one end should be large enough to go over the bait after it has been threaded through the loop on the tackle. The reel line is attached to the loop at the other end as shown in the illustration of page 53. The trace should be furnished with two rustless swivels to allow the bait to spin freely without imparting kink to the line. For light bait casting with the fixed-spool reel the length of the trace need not be more than 2 ft. of 3X gut, looped at one end to go over the bait, and at the other end it should have a double swivel to which the reel line is attached. The longer trace for the Nottingham style reel will require to be equipped with a lead, which serves the triple purpose of carrying out the line, preventing any twist which the swivels might otherwise fail to eliminate from passing into the reel line, and keeping down the minnow to the correct depth in strong water. Various patterns of "anti-kink" leads are available, the general principle of which is that they hang below the line. A simple form consists of a disc of lead doubled saddle-wise over the trace. In light bait spinning no lead on the trace is necessary, that inside the minnow on the Aerial tackle being quite sufficient.

[1] Nylon is now perhaps the most widely used material for spinning lines. (*See notes on pages* 28 *and* 55.)

CHAPTER XV

SPINNING FOR TROUT: METHODS

I PURPOSELY omitted from the last chapter any description of the reels most suitable for spinning as, it seemed to me, their special qualifications are so involved with the casting and manœuvring of the bait that reels and methods can best be dealt with together.

The casual observer might airily sum up the operation something like this: "I don't see anything out of the way about spinning. You just chuck out the bait through the air, and drag it back through the water, and that's all there is to it." Actually there is a good deal more to it.

In casting from a plain revolving reel of the Nottingham type you must estimate fairly accurately the amount of force to be expended in slinging out the weighted tackle in order that that tackle may first overcome the inertia of the drum, then draw off sufficient line to reach the spot aimed at. From this it is obvious that a light, delicately balanced reel is desirable. The Aerial is as good as any and better than most. But the sudden jerk on the reel at the commencement of the cast is liable to cause the drum to pay out line faster than the tackle is carrying it, when an overrun is likely to result in an entanglement. To avoid this the rim of the reel is gently braked by the delicate touch of a sensitive finger. Then again, as the bait approaches the end of its flight it slows down perceptibly, but the whirling drum does not lose its momentum so rapidly, and, unless checked again by the finger, there rapidly ensues a jumbled mess of line by the side of which the intricacies of the Gordian Knot fade into the essence of sweet simplicity.

The tyro attempting to concentrate his mind on these three essential points at the same time may well find himself in a position analogous to that of the raw recruit on his first visit to the range, when he explained his clean miss thus: "First my hand wobbled; then when I'd got my hand steady, the rifle wobbled; and when I'd got both my hand and the rifle steady, the target wobbled".

Human ingenuity, however, has successfully combated this *bête noire*, the over-run, by the invention of reels fitted with mechanical devices—the best known is Allcock's "Easicast"—which render the bugbear practically impossible. The revolving reel should have an optional check, similar to that in a fly reel, which can be slipped off before the cast is made, and slipped on as an aid to playing the fish.

To make the cast with the Nottingham reel the angler should stand with his left shoulder towards the spot aimed at and the baited tackle dangling from the point of the rod. Holding the latter horizontally, it is brought round until it is pointing in a direction opposite to that of the target, the reel being held stationary by pressure of the forefinger upon the rim. In his novitiate the angler will find it expedient to keep his eye on the bait in order to spot the exact moment at which to commence the forward movement. This is at the instant when it reaches the limit of its backward swing. The forward cast is a swinging, forward and upward sweep as the shoulders are brought round towards the goal, the pace increasing to a final swish that puts the elasticity of the rod well into action and speeds the bait on its flight the moment the forefinger releases the drum. If the sympathetic finger is used correctly to counteract the tendency towards an over-run, the bait falls into the water with a straight line, and is spun home by reeling in. If the water is disturbed by current or wind ripples the bait should be spun slowly; in bright, clear water a rather quicker spin will generally be found more effective.

The ideal cast with the Nottingham reel is not acquired in a day. It depends on the correct timing of the various movements, which only diligent practice will assure; but, given that diligent practice and a reasonable amount of intelligence, the whole operation resolves itself gradually into something akin to an automatic process.

In river fishing the cast is usually made across and spun back in a more or less downward curve according to the strength of the current, the last stage of its progress often being upstream under the bank on which the angler is standing. In that case the speed of the recovery of the line should be slackened, as, drawn directly against the stream, the rotation of the bait is otherwise increased more than desirable. Often a trout will follow the lure across the river without making any attempt to take it until speed is eased up at the last lap.

For the type of minnow spinning I have described suitable waters are fairly wide rivers, weir pools, the dancing areas below the shingly bars where tributaries come into the main stream, the slumberous deeps wherein leviathans lurk, and the shady glides under the overhanging trees—if you can induce your bait to restrain its characteristic tendency to form a strong attachment to the branches.

Now, excellent as the Nottingham reel is in many

River Eden, the Home of Bustard Fishing—page 115

CLEAR-WATER WORMING

respects, there is just one thing it will not do—fish the upstream minnow in low clear water after the manner I have generally mentioned in the chapter on "The Fly Rod and the Minnow". For one thing, it will not cast, satisfactorily, a light enough bait—and a light bait is essential to fishing the thin edges of streams no more than a few inches in depth—and for another, it will not recover line fast enough to cause the bait to spin as it is being drawn down the typical stream of a rapid river. Nothing but a geared-up reel will do that.

To fill the gap, early in this century A. Holden Illingworth invented the first fixed-spool "light-casting" reel, and a weird-looking contraption it was, bearing about as much resemblance to an orthodox fishing reel as carrot to a cauliflower. But it did its job, and did it well. How well the following will show.

I knew Illingworth personally and often fished with him. On one occasion we had arranged to meet to try out the first edition of the Illingworth No. 1 on a well-known club water. It was a brilliant day in mid-summer, and the river was so low and clear that it was generally regarded as hopeless, and not another member was out on the water. Illingworth went in at the bottom limit of the length ; I started half a mile higher up. Wading upstream and fishing mainly the rippling runs and shallows at the tails of pools, when, at four o'clock (it was after noon when we commenced to fish), we knocked off and called it a day, we had killed over fifty good trout between us. Had the lust for slaughter been upon us, and had we continued, I have no doubt we could have killed twice as many.

But, do not run away with the idea that those trout had suddenly been affected by a suicidal epidemic; every one of them had been fished for with all the skill and knowledge of which we were capable. And do not be led astray by the erroneous notion that the fixed-spool reel will prove as fatal each and every time it is employed.

In those early days, J. H. R. Bazley, as well as myself, was in close touch with Illingworth, and was keenly interested in the development of the fixed-spool. Well, shortly after the incident I have related I invited Bazley to accompany me for a day's fishing with the new reel on a private length very similar to the water Illingworth and I had fished, and quite as heavily stocked. Again it was a brilliant day, and the conditions, so far as I could judge, were exactly similar to those which prevailed on the club water, and yet, try as we would, we could not touch a fish, and I never came across a man who could handle the fixed-spool better than Bazley, unless it was Illingworth himself. Time after time trout, sometimes three or four at a time, would follow the bait almost to our feet, keeping about a foot behind it, but take it they would not, although we exhausted all our bag-o'-tricks in attempting to induce them to do so. Since then I have found that occasionally they do act like that in low clear water, but why they should I do not know, and the trout won't tell.

A little later Illingworth brought out his No. 2, which resembled in a general way the fixed-spool reels of to-day, and was the grandfather of them all. However much they may differ in details, the best modern fixed-spool reels work on the same fundamental principles. The line is contained on a stationary spool, the axis of which is parallel with the rod, instead of being at right angles to it as in the case of the revolving reel, and the flying bait draws off line exactly in the same manner as you would draw off the thread endways from a reel of cotton.

This obviates any danger of that bugbear, the over-run, but, at the same time, each coil of the line that is drawn off in the manner described puts a turn into the line, and this, if no counteracting influence were brought to bear, would soon kink the line badly. To remedy this the line is rewound on the spool by a flyer, or pick-up, a hook which revolves round the fixed-spool. Thus each revolution of the flyer takes out the same amount of twist as each coil put in in casting. Usually the gear ratio is about three to one, *i.e.* the flyer replaces three coils of the line to one turn of the handle, so a quick recovery is possible.

Another important feature is the slipping clutch, which is adjustable and limits the tension on the line in playing a fish to any degree of strain that may be thought desirable. This reduces breakages to the minimum, for if a fish exerts more power than the clutch is set to resist, all that happens is that the fixed-spool ceases temporarily to justify its name and re-volves, yielding line, but always keeping a heavy steady strain on the fish until the pull of the trout weakens, when the winding-in is resumed.

Some of the less expensive fixed-spool reels, however, are not provided with a flyer. Indeed, they are only fixed-spool as far as the casting is concerned. In re-covering line the spool revolves and takes up the line through a stationary guide. In such cases the spool is reversible and is turned endways about at intervals. It is also to the good to use a bait which spins in a direction opposite to that in which the reel is putting in twist.

The side cast with the fixed-spool reel is, in a way of speaking, the side cast as made with the Nottingham reel, but reproduced on a more delicate scale. There is no swing round of the shoulders, and the action is

almost entirely confined to the wrist. Standing facing
the spot aimed at, the rod is held with the second

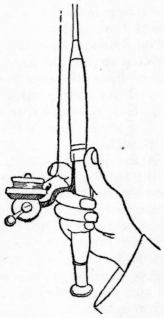

finger close up to the cranked
bracket of the reel (I am
taking the Illingworth No. 3
as typical), while the first
finger, above the bracket, re-
strains the line from slipping
off the spool. At this stage
some anglers hold the line to
the rod with the forefinger.
There is no necessity for this.
It is quite sufficient that the
line be held in the crook of
the forefinger as shown in the
sketch.

With the tackle dangling
from the point, the rod is
gently swung back, and as the
minnow - pendulum reaches
its backward limit, the forward swing — all from the
wrist—is commenced and a
smart flick imparted to it.

GRIP WITH THE FIXED-
SPOOL REEL

The forefinger is straightened, releasing the line, and
away flies the bait to fall gently into the water 20 or
30 yds. away. As it does so, the first turn of the automatic pick-up catches the line preparatory to reeling
in. If the water be of any depth a moment should be
allowed for the minnow to settle down to a suitable
level; if very shallow it should be put in motion at
once, before it has time to get hung up on the bottom.

The side cast is best accomplished with a rod of $7\frac{1}{2}$
to $8\frac{1}{2}$ ft., though in an emergency a $10\frac{1}{2}$ or 11 ft.
stiffish fly rod will do the trick with a fair amount of

success. Of late the American style of casting with a short rod of no more than 5½ ft. or 6 ft. has been adopted by some English light bait spinners. With this weapon the overhead cast is usually employed. Holding the rod erect, the angler gently swings back the dangling bait, and, as it reaches the limit of its outward swing, makes a smart cut forward in a perpendicular plane, imparting a sort of push as he releases the line. In America this cast is usually associated with a multiplying reel which has not yet found too much favour on this side of the Atlantic. (*See note on page* 138.)

The streams, the glassy glides, the gravelly shallows —all may be productive of sport to the upstream minnow fished with a fixed-spool reel in low gin-clear waters under the most brilliant skies if the bait is thrown upward and drawn down a little faster than the current, and it will be almost inevitably found that the fish that fall to the minnow average greater in weight than those that succumb to the blandishments of the fly. Originally, as I have implied, the light-casting fixed-spool reel was introduced for trout fishing in low clear water; but its scope has, since the early Illingworth patents expired, been expanded to cover practically all sorts and conditions of spinning, including fishing for salmon and pike.

There are writers, their pens dipped in venom, who have decried fishing with the fixed-spool reel as a species of legalised crude massacre. Let them try it on the shrunken waters of rapid streams under a blazing August sun, and they will speedily find that it calls for the display of an amount of delicacy and skill greater than is usually shown in fly fishing. I rank it higher than upstream worming, and that is generally classed as one of the fine arts of angling.

There remains another form of spinning the minnow

for trout, and that is trolling, which is described in the chapter on "Lake Fishing".

Another method of trout fishing which has been tried out by a few enthusiastic pioneers bears some resemblance to spinning, but it is not spinning. It is the application to English trout fishing of a method of bass fishing long popular in America and known as plug fishing. The lure, in other words the plug, is a weird-looking object carved out of wood, gaily painted, some-what crudely suggestive of a small fish, and armed with hooks. At rest it floats on the surface, but it is so fashioned that, on being drawn through the water with the line, it dives and wobbles in a manner which the bass find fatally attractive.

The larger forms of plug have been put to the test in salmon and pike fishing on British waters, and have produced encouraging results. Whether the use of the smaller plugs in trout fishing—and some of these small patterns can be fished with a fly rod—is worth while is a matter of opinion. Certainly they will catch trout, and certainly they avoid the kinking of the line, while, further, they do not catch up in the bottom, as spinning tackle is apt to do in shallow water.

NOTE

Multiplying reels have gained considerably in popularity in this country. In principle they are centre-pin reels, but with the handle geared at roughly three to one with the spool. They incorporate a level-wind device to ensure even recovery of the line on to the drum.

CHAPTER XVI

CLEAR-WATER WORMING

THE lowly *Lumbricus*, the despised worm, familiar symbol of worthlessness, does not at first glance start off the casual observer on an ennobling train of thought soaring to the realms of high art; nor, perhaps, does it move him to appreciative recognition of its humble utility. Yet, Gilbert White wrote, "The earth without worms would soon become cold, hard-bound, and void of fermentation; and consequently sterile", and he might have added, had he lived a century later, "and without worms the trout fisher's efforts on the shrunken streams of summer would often prove as sterile".

There is worm fishing *and* worm fishing, and between the two lies all the difference between the most elementary form of angling and a display of skill, combined with a knowledge of river-craft, unsurpassed in few other branches of the sport. Halford himself, keenest of dry-fly enthusiasts, after watching Walbran fish the clear-water worm on the Wharfe, wrote in *The Field*: "A visit to the North with one of the adepts in the art will, beyond doubt, convince the sceptic of the great difference between his preconceived ideas and the reality of clear-water worm fishing". And again: "The points which impressed me most were the strong resemblance between the clear-water worm and dry-fly fishing in respect to the importance of throwing upstream and that of preventing or avoiding drag". With a more intimate acquaintance Halford might have discovered more parallels, or resemblances, between the two arts. Factually the degree of caution often required in stalking the fish in clear-water worming is even greater than that called for in dry-fly fishing, and, at least in my own case, the adoption of the dry-fly fisher's dodge of greasing the line has been found a decided advantage. Figuratively clear-water worming *is* the dry-fly fishing of the worm fisher's craft, and since Stewart demonstrated its possibilities it has gradually won its way to general recognition as one of the highest forms of scientific angling and worthily occupies a niche in the gallery of the piscatorial fine arts.

More or less the upstream worm will kill throughout the season on the rapid rivers, but, as I have written elsewhere, "from about the middle of June until early August may be considered the special period when the trout comes, in low clear water, most readily to that bait, provided the angler's tackle is fine and is manœuvred with finesse. At this time of the year, it may be, a surfeit of insect food has caused the trout's outraged stomach to yearn for a change of diet. From the end of April, and through the greater part of May, it has been battening in the edges of the streams upon the Creepers. Subsequently it has been taking heavy toll of the Stone-fly—not to mention side dishes of Duns and Spinners—and its appetite, cloyed with the unlimited richness of Stone-fly toffee to breakfast, and Stone-fly toffee to dinner, and Stone-fly toffee to tea, hails the appearance of such a 'cut off the plain joint' as a worm in the light of a welcome relief."

Certain it is that under the blazing skies of summer, when the rivers run low and gin-clear, and sweltering humanity's notions of idyllic pastoral bliss hover fondly round some umbrageous bosky retreat with a long

TYPICAL STONE-FLY WATER

May-fly Dapping in Lough Corrib

cooling drink in it, the clear-water worm fisher looks for his richest harvest, but he has got to bring industry and dexterity to bear on the job. He has got to work hard for his results; his is no gentle dalliance

> In the Valley of "What's the use"?
> In the Province of "Let her slide",
> Where the "old tired feeling" is in the air,
> In the home of the listless "I don't care",
> Where the "Put it offs" abide,

as some anonymous poet has sung.

Naturally, the amount of energy required for the successful day's fishing with the clear-water worm depends on the nature of the water exploited. The gentler streams may be negotiated without excessive exertion, but after a man has crawled and scrambled and clawed and climbed over four or five miles of rugged upland river-bed, he may realise something of the estatic joy of the mountaineer when, at the end of a perfect day, he exclaims: "Every muscle aching like a general infirmary! Feet pounded into ragged masses of painful pulp! Shan't be able to lift a limb again for a week! Another hundred yards of it, and it would have killed me outright! What a heavenly climb it has been!"

Of course, the less strenuous will eschew such delights, and confine his attentions to the easier gradients of the lower, but still streamy, reaches.

Nor must it be supposed that during the period I have mentioned the trout will invariably prove responsive to the skilfully offered worm. I have known them at times to go off the bait as suddenly as at times they will cease to rise to the fly. One instance I particularly remember. A friend and myself were fishing a delectable private length that was full of fish. In the first twenty minutes we killed 17 trout. It seemed as though the fish had been seized with a midsummer madness that impelled them to get caught with as little delay as possible, and, of course, we accommodated them. Then they mysteriously went clean off the worm. They simply would not have it no matter how seductively it was presented. At times, in the shade of the trees and where the angle of light was right for permitting us to see into the depth of the stream for 10 yds. ahead, I watched the bait swim close past trout after trout without attracting the slightest attention, and I could almost hear them sniff contemptuously: "Humph! That worm is sour!"

Although we continued fishing for some hours, we only added three trout to the bag.

While, as a rule, the clear-water worm will kill in summer throughout the day, there is no doubt that the cream of the sport can be skimmed in the early morning, say any time between sun-up and nine o'clock. Then through the dew-drenched pastures the knowing one makes his way to his favourite stream, a flannel bag, containing a gross of well-scoured worms in damp moss, hanging open-mouthed from a waist-coat buttonhole, or from a ring in front of the pannier strap, in readiness for baiting.

On the choice of worms opinions differ widely; but it may be taken as a general rule that in clear water the trout will most readily come to a bright red or pink wriggler, in accordance with the theory that in clear water they hunt by sight and are more easily attracted by a dainty, well-scoured charmer ablush with "that schoolgirl complexion" than by the brandling with its more sober appearance and evil-smelling nastiness. I say "generally", for there are occasions when the reverse is the case, and there are clear-water worm fishers who prefer brandlings. F. M. ("Max") Walbran, one of the best clear-water worm fishers I ever knew, confessed to a partiality for brandlings; but, as they do not toughen well in scouring, and, consequently, are more liable to part from the hooks in casting, he usually fished with maiden dew worms.

These are small varieties of the common or garden lob. They scour well and to a fairly decent colour, and are easily obtained. Those from 2½ in. to 3 in. should be selected. I have used them as often as any other sort, and they have done well for me. But, there is another kind, sometimes called the "button" worm, that I like better. It is found when turning up hard, dryish ground, where it loves to lie coiled and tangled up in a ball. It is often a tempting coral colour when found, and scours to a delicate pink. Taking it by and large, and without indulging in a confusing dissertation on the rival merits of "blueheads", "Edinburgh pink-tails", etc. etc., what are wanted are worms of about 3 in. in length that are, or will scour, red and are fairly tough.

Having caught your worms, the next thing is to scour them. This is most handily done by lightly packing a large earthenware plant-pot with clean damp moss. I prefer the kind known, I think, as "stag's horn", which grows plentifully in forest glades, and among the grass in poor meadows and on hedgebanks. But first be sure that you place a bit of slate or flat stone over the hole in the bottom of the pot to ensure that the worms do not play truant by slipping out at the back door. Place the worms on the top of the moss, cover with a tile or board, and, in the cleansing process, they will work through the moss to the bottom of the pot. The next day, having prepared a second pot of similar dimensions in the same way as the first, remove the dirt and debris from the upper layer of the first pot, and invert that receptacle on the second. The worms will then work their way down into the moss of the second pot, when the contents of the first can be washed, and a little fresh moss added, in readiness to repeat the process as before. At the end of four days the worms should be cleaned and toughened ready for use.

Now for the tackle: You may use a single No. 6, round bend, cranked-shank hook, inserting the point of the hook a little below the head of the worm, and threading the wriggler up the shank, so that, with its head drawn over the crank to prevent its slipping down, its tail is left to waggle freely. North of the Border the 3-hook Stewart tackle may, perhaps, be first favourite; but elsewhere the 2-hook Pennell tackle is probably more popular. In this arrangement two No. 3 hooks are whipped on the gut, 1 in. or $1\frac{1}{2}$ in. apart, with red silk. The upper hook is passed laterally through the worm just below its head, the lower one 1 in. above its tail. Some anglers give the worm a turn round the gut between the upper and lower hooks; but, personally, I generally leave the bait free to wriggle at its own sweet will between the two points of attachment. It seems to me that it looks more natural, and as if it were enjoying itself, as it comes trundling down the stream.

Also, in place of whipping on the hooks, I tie on a couple of No. 3, straight-eyed hooks Pennell fashion, the lower one secured at the end of the cast with a Turle knot, the higher one threaded on the bight of a simple thumb, or overhand, knot and drawn tight. This is a faulty arrangement, and yet, paradoxical as it may appear, there is virtue in its faultiness. In upstream worm fishing the gut—especially drawn gut—frays badly and quickly through friction with the stones. Consequently, unless you are asking for trouble, the hooks should be stripped from the frayed part at intervals, and re-tied on the cast a few inches higher up. But, through forgetfulness or recklessness, you are apt to omit to attend to this little safety-first precaution until it is too late and a hooked fish has left you lamenting.

Now, with the tied and eyed tackle I have described, the upper hook is capable of holding the average trout you are likely to encounter without the knot shifting its position. But if you come to grips with an outsize fish on the upper hook, that thumb-knot is liable to run down the gut until it is stopped by the lower hook. You do not lose your fish, but you are then bound to cut off those hooks and mount them afresh.

Nine feet is the usual length for the cast, which is tapered to 3X or 4X. At one time I used to think that this degree of fineness was essential to complete success in clear-water worm fishing; I am not so sure about it now. Some years ago a firm of tackle dealers sent me for trial a couple of fine undrawn casts. I used no other for upstream worming that summer, and there was no apparent diminution in the size of my catches, while the undrawn gut did not fray so quickly as the drawn. Still, I confess that I have on most occasions fished with the tapered drawn cast, for the simple reason that I have always had a supply of that description handy for fly fishing.

In the early days of clear-water worming on the Border rivers, *i.e.* in Stewart's time, double-handed trout rods were in common use, and Stewart himself recommended that the weapon "should not be shorter than from fourteen to sixteen feet", while rods of even greater length were employed. To-day the ideal rod for the purpose is a light, single-handed whole-cane one of 12 ft., with a split-cane or greenheart top tapering to a delicate degree of elasticity, and the same tool is also admirably adapted to Creeper fishing. With long rods it is much easier, with no more line out than little in excess of the length of the rod, to lob, or pitch, the bait with an underhand swing to a fishing distance in a quick stream; but a great many upstream wormers make good shift with the $10\frac{1}{2}$-ft. stiffish fly rod common on the rivers they haunt, with which they can, at will, change over to fly fishing should the conditions suggest such an alteration of tactics.

No special line or reel is required; those used in fly fishing will serve as well as any, and wading is, with very few exceptions, the only means of approaching the fish undetected.

Commencing, say, a few yards below the point where the dancing stream bubbles over a shingly bar to find restful peace for a while in the slumberous pool below, the angler slips quietly into the edge of the dub, draws off 18 ft. or more of line, and, with what manner of cast he may favour, drops the unshotted bait, unobtrusively, in the foot of the rapid, to be trundled as to the manner born and with no suspicious haste over the bar of gravel below which, in the slackening undercurrent, trout lie in wait with an eye ever lifting for what they may devour. Searching this section of water just below where the current tumbles over the ridge of pebbles, the angler by and by detects a stoppage of the line, pauses a moment, and strikes. It may be, it often is, that his hooks have caught up on a submerged stone, but this time luck is with him, and the next moment he is playing a lively $\frac{1}{2}$-pounder in the head of the pool.

Across the head of the dub, out of the full force of

the entering stream, is a shallow, feebly eddying slack that laps a gravelly shore. Ten to one there is a trout there. Owing to the intervening depth of water it may require a longish line to reach it, but the attempt is well worth while. Up and across flies the uncurling line to drop the worm, with no more than the merest apology of a splash, at the spot aimed at, and the waiting trout annexes it instantly. One jump it makes as it feels the steel, and comes flip-flopping across the head of the pool to the landing-net.

Now, wading upward and keeping 3 or 4 yds. from the near bank, our angler proceeds to fish the stream itself, perhaps shortening his line to 15 ft. or so, if the current is rapid. Here he drops his bait lightly in the very edge of the quick water, which is so shallow that the uninitiated would not dream there was sufficient depth to cover a fish; but it is just in this fringe of the current that the upstream wormer may look for his best sport. Gently the worm drifts down as the rod top is slowly raised—not too quickly, or that would drag the bait into suspicious haste and put the fish on the *qui vive*. Possibly by the time the worm has travelled a couple of yards, if the fates are propitious, the line stops. Again comes a short pause to allow the fish to mouth the worm, and as the line tightens there is the flash of a golden side in the ripples, a dart into the heavier water, and a madcap trout is capering down the surface of the rapid like an aquatic devil-among-the-tailors. The novice is advised to let the hooked fish go past—always keeping a reasonably tight line—and play it out in the water below. But the old-timer submerges his landing-net in the path of the cavorting trout as it comes prancing along, and lifts it out.

If the stream be a narrow one, the angler may wade up the middle of it, fishing the opposite edges alternately, and trying a few casts between-whiles in the intervening area. But if the stream be a wide one, then he should fish up one side, trying the water from the extreme edge to mid-stream, after which he should come back and fish up the other side.

A little bay, formed in the lee of a tiny spit of pebbles, is a very likely lie, and here the worm is tossed close to, but slightly above, the point whence the current shoulders it into the quieter water and, maybe, into the ken of a fish in an accommodating mood. The eddy behind an upstanding boulder is another good spot; but the worm is not cast into the eddy, rather into the rapid water that laves the side of the boulder. Down this run the bait comes trundling, and the trout behind the boulder makes a dart at it. Or yonder, the boulders have served to form a small rocky basin with a flow little more than a trickle through it. The bait is unostentatiously dropped into that trickle above its point of entry, to be carried through the snug retreat in the hope of picking the watery pocket of its contents.

The "hang" of the stream—the shallow, glassy glide at the tail of the pool above, where the water gathers speed—holds trout, and is worth prospecting carefully as in upstream wet-fly fishing. This water being crystal-clear and unbroken, a longer line will be found useful, say sufficient length to reach a spot 30 ft. from where the angler is standing, as the fish are here more difficult of approach, and extra caution is called for, even to crouching low and occasionally kneeling in the water. But, sooner or later, perseverance is rewarded and a good fish or two added to the tale of the slain.

And so the game goes on, all the likely spots receiving due attention—the edges of the streams, the little eddies, the runs among the upstanding boulders, the

148

quieter, deeper runs under the banks and the over-hanging branches where the worm can be cajoled into such promising lies. Even the heavy currents in mid-stream will often yield a few good fish, but it may in such cases be necessary to nip a shot on the line to bring the bait down within notice of the trout.

On the question of using shot on the line in clear-water worm fishing, opinions differ somewhat. In the main it is held—and I heartily endorse the doctrine —that no shot should be used save when fishing the heavy currents or when the angler is faced with a strong downstream wind. Such a breeze may not only render the casting of the bait upstream difficult, but after the cast has been accomplished the wind, blowing back the line, is apt to impart objectionable drag to the worm in its progress downstream. The addition of a shot, distinctly, as an upstream veteran once put it to me, "helps the worm forrard", and, further, acts as a break in checking its tendency to outspeed the current.

While some of the text-books strongly advocate the swinging underhand pitch forward in worm fishing, which is only practicable when using a short line, the majority of upstream wormers I have seen—and I have seen a great many from the days of Pritt and Walbran onward—employ the same casts, both under-hand and overhead, as in fly fishing, with a slight, but important, difference. Weighted with a worm, the movement is much more slow and deliberate, and if either of these casts be used a more distinct pause is made at the end of the back cast to allow the line to be fully extended before the forward throw is com-menced, otherwise the worm is very liable to part company with the hooks. When a wide, curving, con-tinuous cast is made there is no necessity for the pause, as nothing in the nature of a jerk is imparted to it. To avoid unnecessary splash as the worm enters the water, the forward cast should conclude with a forward thrust to the full extent of the arm just before the bait reaches its goal.

I have often read in angling books that, in fishing the upstream worm, the rod point should be raised so that nothing but the cast is in the water. Unless the angler be fishing practically under his rod point this is more easily said than done, and it is an everyday practice of the North Country man to fish the worm with 20 ft. or more of line extended from the rod point. Unnecessary slack is certainly to be avoided, and this can be assured by rubbing the reel line well with a flotant, as in dry-fly fishing and in fishing the wet fly upstream as previously described. Further, this renders the progress of the line more easily seen, and a stoppage detected. I adopted this method many years ago, and I have had no reason to complain of its inefficiency.

Upstream worming entails a lot of rough going, and the landing net with the 5 ft. shaft, shod with steel hook and spike, which can be used as a wading staff, is often a valuable accessory.

It is possible to fish the clear-water worm with the "thread line" and fixed-spool reel. To the best of my belief, I was the first to try it in the early days of the Illingworth No. 1, which was then in very few hands; but I soon reverted to the use of the weapons I have mentioned—12-footer and 10½-ft. fly rod—with a 9-ft. fly rod for small burns, as a pleasanter, and more profitable, practice. Excellent as the fixed-spool reel is for many styles of fishing, it is far from its best in upstream worming.

CHAPTER XVII

THICK-WATER WORMING

WORM fishing in thick water is mostly practised on the moorland rivers and their tributaries, subject, as they are, to spells of drought broken by rousing spates, while the chalk streams pursue the even tenor of their way in comparatively undisturbed serenity.

Thick-water worming is, on these moorland streams, the end-all and be-all of the typical "local" who fishes with his eye on the pot, while his dame takes a sympathetic interest in his efforts and keeps the frying-pan handy. Not for him are the subtle joys of delicately cocking a floater over the neb of a hypercritical fish, nor the ethereal delights of scrambling laboriously over miles of rugged river-bed to stalk the quick-eyed quarry in the shrunken trickles. He prefers to take his fishing sitting down—literally or figuratively.

Take a peep at his native hamlet. For weeks it has drowsed in sun-seared apathy, under summer skies, to the murmuring lullaby of the shrunken stream. Once or twice an alien has invaded the Sleepy Hollow, armed with weirdly fragile tackle, and has charmed a brace or two of trout from the attenuated trickles and contracted pools by the plying of his occult arts; but such feats of legerdemain are regarded with phlegmatic toleration, without awakening any desire for emulation.

The village merely turns over languidly, and goes to sleep again, until, one fine morning, the doctor's car returns from a visit far up the vale and runs a pin into it. A cloudburst over the distant hills has transformed the upper feeders into raging torrents, the river is coming down in spate and within an hour or so there will be a "fishing water". The word goes round like the Fiery Cross calling to arms. The village has suddenly leapt into activity. The joiner downs his tools, the cobbler deserts his last and calls it a day. In an hour the harvest of the river will be ripe for the fishing-rod, and nothing else matters. It is even told that in one village, and on such an occasion, a funeral was suddenly postponed on the plea that "grandad can wait for a day, and this fishing water won't".

Hither and thither men with spades and forks hurry in the breathless hunt for worms. Garden plots are savagely turned over; antique manure heaps are raided. Ancient rods are unearthed from outhouses, or taken down from the nails upon which they have reposed on the beams of barns—rods fitted with old-time brass pirns furnished with cord lines—and the race for the favoured corners begins. The tackle is often of the crudest—huge hooks on thick gut, baited with a bunch of two or three worms, and heavily weighted. Sometimes a rude form of paternoster is used, fitted with two hooks and a plummet.

Soon the river is running bank high with a rolling, turbid flood, and through the hours the patient "locals" sit, or stand, and fish at their stations, until, in the waning afternoon, they return triumphant to their homes with their speckled spoils strung through the gills on an osier twig. Then the frying-pans come into requisition, and the sweet incense of sizzling trout ascends to high heaven from a contented hamlet.

In the polite literature of the angle rod it is customary to anathematise fishing with worm for trout in flood water as an abomination, harmful to a fishery, and totally unworthy of being classed as sportsmanlike. Undeniably, it is a legal method of catching trout. Certainly it is not, as usually practised, one of the most scientific branches of the gentle craft; but whether it be sportsmanlike or the reverse depends upon the angler. Personally, when I have found the river brimming with a brown, blinding flood, I have spent enjoyable hours in fishing the thick-water worm, and have never felt one twinge of conscience; but, then, I have never fished thus except with a fly rod and the same fine gut, 3X or 4X, I should have employed in fly fishing. Granted, it is easier to hook a trout in thick water; but, on the other hand, it is more difficult to land it on fine tackle once, in its first moment of panic, it darts off into the heart of the galloping current and you have both trout and heavy stream to play.

Here is an incident I once witnessed that etched a lasting picture on my memory. The river was in flood, with three or four feet of thick brown "fresh" surging down its course. I was standing on a high tree-fringed bank, looking down through the leafy maze at the slacker water under the bank, when an old angler toddled up, and observed quietly: "There's a trout down there for a fiver".

"And it's likely to stop there", I returned. He did not reply. He was armed with a split-cane fly rod, his ordinary fly line, and a 3-yds. drawn-gut cast, shotted and baited with worm. Calmly, imperturbably, he wound up line until the shot was at the point of his rod. Then he deliberately inserted rod point and dangling tackle into that bewildering entanglement of boughs and twigs and leaves, and I thought he had gone clean mad. However, carefully and with no undue haste he skilfully dodged all obstructions to left and right and fore and aft, until—miraculously, it seemed to me—the bait reached the water without fouling anything.

Even then there did not appear to me to be the most forlorn hope of getting a fish; for there was barely a couple of yards of water clear of obstruction in the way of boughs awash in the flood. If a trout took him it looked like a dead certainty there would be a smash; but the old hand never batted an eyelid. Quietly he let off three or four yards of line, and within a couple of minutes he had a trout on the hook. It was a lively ¾-pounder, and he played that fish to a dead standstill with the rod top a yard under water to avoid fouling the half-submerged branches. Eventually he reeled it in until he had it just under the point of his rod, then, just as coolly as ever, he insinuated his long-handled landing-net into that intricate jungle, worked his trout into it, and complacently withdrew rod and landing-net together. It was one of the most astonishing bits of pure artistry I ever saw displayed in the catching of trout, and that, if you please, was thick-water worming.

As in clear-water worming, opinions differ as to the best kind of worm for this style of fishing. Almost any variety will do at a pinch, though I think the brandling is the most attractive and I have an idea that it possesses its greatest charm in flood water when it is used unscoured with all its native fragrance thick upon it. Unfortunately, it is then more tender and liable to break away from the hook. Either Pennell, Stewart or single-hook tackle may be used, and the amount of shot nipped on the gut should be, as nearly as can be judged, sufficient to sink the worm and allow it to trundle gently along the bottom—that is, if you are fishing without float, as the majority of thick-water worm fishers do.

On waters where it is a common practice to swim the worm for winter grayling, the same tackle is frequently used for trout in flood water—a tiny round cork, about the size of a marble, adjusted so that the worm, above which suitable shot are nipped on, should swim nicely clear of the bottom.

If a single hook be used, then that hook should be of the "sliced" variety, i.e. a tiny spur is cut to project upward and outward from the back of the shank, or of the "cranked-shank" pattern, in which the shank projects a little above the whipping and is turned outward. In both cases the worm, drawn over these special features, is prevented from sagging "all of a heap", like a garterless stocking, on the bend.

The best places to fish are the slacker water under the banks, the eddies, the sheltered spots in the V where, here and there, the heavy current splits, the backwaters in close proximity to the main stream, the quieter tails of pools, and, close to the bank, the swims immediately below where the tributaries come in. Further, where the swollen rapid flows over a wide shingly bed with gently shelving sides, a few good trout may often be secured by running the shotted worm down the edges of the current.

Thick-water worm fishers are not entirely agreed as to the stage of the flood at which the fish take the bait most eagerly. Many hold that they bite best in the rising water; some that the golden opportunity comes as the flood begins to wane. The inveterate worm fisher solves the problem by fishing the swollen stream all the time, so that he is bound to catch it at its best. In these days of extensive drainage a moorland river quickly rises, and quickly runs down, first to a minnow water, then to a fly water.

CHAPTER XVIII

STONE-FLY AND CREEPER FISHING

EVEN in Cotton's time the Stone-fly and the Green Drake were rival claimants to the title of "May-fly"; and he bracketed them as "the matadores for trout and grayling, and in their season kill more fish in our Derbyshire rivers than all the rest, past and to come, in the whole year besides". The title is still applied to the Stone-fly on the rapid rivers of the Northern Counties and on the Scottish streams where it abounds, a practice which is apt to cause confusion when anglers from different districts forgather.

And to a great extent, to justify its claim to May-fly honours, the Stone-fly plays on the moorland rivers a part very similar to that of the Drake on the dry-fly streams. Kingsley wrote of the trout during the May-fly rise: "Poor carnal parties! Why shouldn't they tuck while they can? May-flies come to them at Whitsuntide as club feasts do to the clods, to give them one jolly blow-out in the year, and it's a pleasure to look at them." Kingsley, of course, had in mind the hatch of Drakes on the chalk streams; but his words are equally applicable to the annual appearance of the Stone-fly on the stony-bedded North Country rivers, and the gusto with which the fish gorge on that dainty, what time, after subsisting through the earlier weeks of spring on a less bountiful diet, they plump themselves out in a manner recalling the old aldermanic banqueting rule of commencing the feast 8 in. from the table and eating until the waistcoat touched the mahogany. The trout of these moorland rivers only reach the pink of culinary perfection and fighting fettle after they have freely fed on the Stone-fly and, in that fly's larval form, the Creeper.

On the Northern rivers the fly is due to appear about the 20th of May, but for a month previous to that the fish have been feeding, in gradually increasing rations, on the Creeper, which during the earlier portion of its larval existence lurks snugly under the stones in the deeper parts and is not readily accessible. But with the growth of the propagatory urge, it commences to work its way to the edges of the stony streams, preparatory to its emergence from the water for the purpose of shedding its shuck and appearing as the mature insect. And it is during this preparatory stage that the trout love to hunt it in the thin margins of the streams.

Cotton was guilty of the indiscretion of referring incidentally to the beauty of the Stone-fly. It is not beautiful—except, perhaps, in the eye of the trout. It makes no dazzling splosh in Nature's decorative scheme. Actually it consists, in the case of the female, of an inch and a quarter of drab ugliness, with yellow-ringed body, dark-veined drab wings folded flat upon its back, and a pair of stubby anterior whisks protruding from its western extremity like the prongs of a carving-fork. The wings of the female are long, covering the whole of the body, and provide the means of a lumbering sort of flight; but those of the male are short rudimentary affairs that are useless for aerial service. Consequently, the male, or "jack", as it is called, is always to be found at home in the chinks of the stones, or under them, close to the edge of the water; while the female flaunts itself abroad, sunning itself on the riverside walls and fences. The Stone-fly is the largest of our aquatic insects, and, once seen, its identity cannot be mistaken.

Much ingenuity has been expended on attempts to produce artificial Stone-flies that would defy the critical discernment of the trout—but with such indifferent success that the practice of using the natural insect as a lure remains supreme. John Jackson, the author of *The Practical Fly Fisher*, who was born and lived all his life on the banks of a famous Yorkshire Stone-fly river, the Yore, gave this dressing:

Body.—Two strands of yellow, and one of drab ostrich herl, neatly ribbed; tie with brown silk.

Wings.—Feather from the inside of a grey Goose's wing.

Legs.—Brown hackle.

Horns and Tail.—Rabbit's whiskers.

But he confessed, "The May-fly is generally fished natural, being large enough to swim a good sized hook, or two smaller ones tied double. . . . An imitation of so large a fly can scarcely be expected to kill except in a wind, or late in the evening."

A supply of bait can be obtained by turning over the stones near the edge of the stream, but nimble fingers are required for the job, as, to put it in the words of a friend, "the critters, if they are no great shakes on flying, are particularly handy with their feet". The collected flies may be stored in some suitable receptacle overnight. Tackle dealers market special boxes for the purpose. My own Stone-fly box, with which I have no fault to find, is a very simple affair, consisting of a four-ounce flat tobacco tin having a hinged lid. Several small ventilation holes are pricked in the top and sides, and a bigger hole, sufficiently large to take a small medicine-bottle cork, is bored in one end. As each fly is captured it is popped in through this hole and the cork replaced. When you require one for bait you simply remove the cork and a fly obligingly walks out into the waiting hand, when you replace the cork before a second emerges. On no account open the lid when the Stone-flies are inside. If you do an instantaneous jail-delivery will ensue, the released prisoners swarming "all over the shop", and considerable exasperation will be generated before their recapture is effected. I should add that, to avoid leaving a sharp edge round the orifice, the hole at the end of the box should first be cut much smaller than it is ultimately intended to be, then enlarged to the proper size by rotating in it a blunt, tapered instrument. This turns in the edge o. the tin and leaves a smooth entrance for the cork. Nothing in the shape of moss or other fancied creature-comfort should be placed in the box. The Stone-fly needs nothing to nurture or entertain it during its period of confinement.

Anglers are not entirely agreed as to whether the long-winged, larger female insect, or the smaller, short-jacketed jack proves the most killing bait, though the majority, with whose opinion I am in accord, favour the former. It is argued that the female, with its wider expanse of wing, not only floats better but causes a greater flutter on the surface of the water, and is, therefore, more easily spotted by the trout. Against this it is urged that more fish are missed in striking on account of the bait being seized by the wings and dragged off the hooks before the entire fly is taken in the mouth. As a remedy for this some anglers trim a little from the wings of the female, with the scissors, before baiting with it.

As a comparison of old methods with modern usages, I might mention that our great-grandfathers seem to have confined their Stone-fly fishing mostly to bushing, dibbing or bobbing, as it is variously called. It was the method advocated by Cotton, and in a quaint old manuscript treatise that fell into my hands some years ago, an illiterate North Country fisherman writes: "Abought the First of June you may Seek for the May Flies which you will fiend under the Stones upon the Gravel Beds you will fiend them Very Near to the Water Edge you Must Take the Largest size you Must Bob with them under the Bushes as you will not Like to wade up the Streams Fish with a No. 5 Hook Tied upon strong Gutt use a Short Line to Bob with about 30 Inches long put the Hook Through the Shoulders of the Flie".

At odd times, when the lazy fit has been upon me and an accommodating breeze has been blowing upstream, I have killed trout on the Stone-fly by adopting the principles of Green Drake dappers, to the extent of inserting ten or a dozen yards of floss silk between my cast and the reel line. Then at an upward lift of the rod point the line goes bellying out upstream and is so manœuvred that the bait falls gently in the vicinity of the spot aimed at, and comes drifting down the current until, happily, it is intercepted by a waiting fish.

Anything in the nature of dibbing with the Stone-fly has in later days, however, largely given way to the more scientific and sporting method of fishing the bait upstream on light tackle pretty much as one would fish the artificial fly. How effective this method may be the reader can judge from the following extract from the late Captain Frank Chapman's book on *The Gun, Rod and Rifle*: "By far the heaviest bags of trout I have killed have been with the stone fly. . . . Starting with my faithful man (Loftus) at six o'clock in the morning under West Burton waterfall (in Wensleydale) and fished up to Walden to where the road crosses the beck not far from the top of the Dale. I left off at three o'clock. The muscles of my right forearm had quite given out, as well they might; even then, however, the trout were still on it as keen as ever. I do not know the exact weight of the trout, but they numbered over two hundred, and being, I should say, not more than four to the pound on the average, they must have weighed nearly fifty pounds. I had three panniers all filled, my man had both the inside pockets of his shooting coat full, and also some in the landing-net."

The orthodox tackle takes the form of a couple of small hooks whipped with yellow silk on opposite sides of the end of a link of fine gut. The lower hook may be No. 2 or No. 3, and the upper hook No. 1. These should be about ⅝ in. apart. Frequently, when I have happened to be out of this special tackle, I have improvised with a couple of small-eyed hooks tied on the end of the cast as for upstream worm fishing, and they have proved a serviceable makeshift. The lower, larger hook is passed downward through the abdomen of the fly, the upper hook upward through the head. The ordinary fly cast of 3 yds., tapered to 3X or 4X, with the fly rod of 10½ or 11 ft. and waterproofed silk fly line, is usually employed, though the 12-ft. rod, such as described in connection with clear-water worming, may possess a few advantages on wide rivers.

As the trout are most numerous in the very edges of the streams, hunting the Creepers which have not yet come ashore, and eagerly on the lookout for any Stone-fly which may, through misadventure, have got into the water, it is in these streamy margins that lick the gravel shore that the angler looks for his briskest sport. And, should the river be running boldly, but not in flood, with a few inches of fresh water—just sufficient to wash the newly hatched flies from their waterside retreats into the stream, and thereby put the fish ravenously on the feed—he may well have justification in regarding the occasion as his busy day.

Wading upstream, he casts his bait lightly ahead—taking care to avoid anything in the nature of a jerk, for the Stone-fly is a fragile morsel and easily divorced from the hooks—to fall softly on the thin water that skirts the central current. Down it comes fluttering invitingly on the surface until, perchance, it is quietly sucked under, or it disappears in a sudden boil. A distinct pause is allowed before the strike is made, and, if that strike has not been too hasty, a rollicking $\frac{1}{2}$-pounder is quickly netted.

While, as I have said, the briskest sport may be expected in the margins of the streams, not *all* the trout are there collected, and the favoured spots named in the chapter on "Clear-water Worming" should be given a trial.

Thus far I have written of the sport as it is usually pursued when the angler is favoured with, for summer, at least a generous water. But, to me, Stone-fly fishing is far more fascinating when the river is low and clear. Prodigious baskets need not then be looked for, but a nice dish of 6 to 10 brace may often be secured when the average practitioner would deem the water not worth fishing, and that by adopting dry-fly tactics; indeed, the method employed *is* dry-fly fishing with the natural insect instead of the artificial.

You may, with greased line, fish the rise by—after stealthily stalking your fish—dropping the Stone-fly 18 in. above its nose and allowing it to float down without drag, when, if all happens right, it vanishes in the vortex of a widening dimple and the battle is joined. Or, on the pools and gentle glides, you may fish the spots where the fish *ought* to be with like agreeable results. The once dancing streams, attenuated to lazy murmuring trickles, will yield a fish or two, and the deeper water under the tree-fringed banks, if you can get your fly on it, gives good returns.

A few precocious specimens of the Stone-fly may be met with in the earlier days of May, or even in April, but the main hatch comes on in the last ten days or so of the merry month and, normally, continues over the first week in June. Should, however, a rousing spate come along while the main hatch is at its height, sweeping away the newly hatched fly in myriads, the season may end prematurely there and then.

The Creeper, the larva of the Stone-fly, may be, so far as outward appearance goes, described as a Stone-fly without wings. It is a killing bait from the latter part of April until the mature fly appears, and is fished on the same tackle as the fly, but with the difference that the former is an underwater lure while the latter is fished on the surface; consequently, when fishing the heavier streams with the Creeper it is often advisable to nip a small shot on the gut a few inches above the bait to sink it to the required depth. Some of the Creepers are almost black in colour, while others are olive with the under side of the abdomen yellow, and for some reason the trout appear to prefer the "yellow bellies". Undoubtedly they find them succulent morsels. One keeper told me they "taste sweetish". I took his word for it.

To obtain a supply for bait it is usually recommended that you should stand in the edge of a quick stream, holding your fine-meshed landing-net bow downwards in the current a yard or so below you. You then perform a sort of vigorous double-shuffle with your feet among the submerged stones. This dislodges the Creepers from their retreats, whereupon they are swept along into the net before they can recover their footing, and can be picked out of the net. A far, far better thing, to my way of thinking, is to bribe some enterprising youngsters with a few coppers to harvest a supply for you. Once gathered, the Creepers may be kept and carried in the box you use for transporting the Stone-fly, but, when the former are to be the inmates, the box should be lined with damp moss.

It is little use to fish the Creeper otherwheres than in the streams. As Stewart wrote: "Whereas the angler will frequently catch trout with the worm in moderately still water, he will scarcely ever catch one with the creeper, and should therefore confine his operations to strong water". In other words, Creeper fishing closely resembles fishing the streams with the clear-water worm.

When trout are whole-heartedly on the Creeper rampage on such typical Stone-fly rivers as Eden, Wharfe, Yore, Tees, and the Border streams, it is seldom they can be induced to look with the eye of desire at anything else. I have known a skilful angler fish the upstream worm blank; while on the same river, on the next length below, another has been filling his creel with the assistance of the Creeper.

CHAPTER XIX

DAPPING WITH THE MAY-FLY AND "DADDY"

IF the itinerant angler would sample Irish trout fishing when, as a Hibernian friend put it, "all the fun of the *fario* is mighty convaynient for the holiday angler who does not care to exert himself too much", he should visit one or other of the favoured western loughs during the latter half of May or the earlier part of June. Then, the blow-line fishing is in full swing, and, given a boatman who knows his job, an indulgent breeze, and the trout in an accommodating humour, he will have no cause to envy kings or princes.

It has been told that to a proud, long-lineaged American dame, boasting of her family tree whose roots were embedded in the earliest traditions, it was suggested that, probably, she could trace her ancestry to some forbear who was in the Ark with Noah, when she snorted indignantly: "With Noah? That crush? I'd hand it to you good and plenty, sir, that the Van Busters always had a yacht of their own!"

Now, while the Irish waters provide an amazing variety of angling such as is habitually practised in other lands, they may almost claim blow-line fishing with the May-fly as "a yacht of their own", so to speak, and a sound craft, too, for those who, in the genial warmth of early summer, do not hanker after the strenuous life. On a typical lough, and under favourable conditions, dapping with the Green Drake is a summer idyll punctuated with hectic splashes.

For, not only are trout of average dimensions to be encountered with more than ordinary frequency, but the sockdolagers, which at other times prowl about the depths, taking heavy toll of their juvenile relatives and ignoring the light confectionery of entomological dainties, now rise to higher things, and it is no rare thing for the May-fly dapper to top up his catch with a 5- or 6-pounder. Larger fish are at times taken, and here is a curious coincidence: According to Jock Scott's *Game Fish Records*, the biggest trout caught in Lough Corrib on the dap was one of $13\frac{1}{2}$ lb., killed on June 11th, 1914; and the biggest caught in Lough Derg was precisely the same weight, and was caught in the same season.

Idly your boat drifts along before the caressing zephyr, as, from the top ring of your long bamboo rod the floss silken line bellies in the kindly breeze, carrying at its other end a couple of natural May-flies impaled upon a hook, and you humour the situation by raising or lowering your rod point, so that the bait rides the laughing ripples as jauntily as though there were no string to it and you had nothing, not even a laugh, up your sleeve.

Here and there unattached Green Drakes swim the dancing wavelets like miniature fairy barks. Here is one! And the next minute it isn't. Gone like the snow-flake in the river. Another minute, and your daintily skimming bait has done the vanishing act in the vortex of a tiny swirl. But don't run away with the notion that these trout, even in the May-fly season, are fired with any vaulting ambition to hook them-selves, or that, having hooked themselves, they are going to jump straight into the angler's pannier. Many escape through the angler yielding to the instinctive impulse to strike at once, which is the common cause of failure. Instead, you should curb impatience by deliberately murmuring some such formula as "Half a mo'. And now we show!"

Then you strike—not as though you were trying to "knock him for six"—just a steady but decisive tightening of the line after, as my boatman expressed it, you have "given the gintleman time to git the ironmongery well into his mouth". And if it be one of the hefty, "rip-raring" swashbucklers of the lough you are into, your heart will be in your mouth—when it isn't in your boots—and life will be one ecstatic thrill until you have cajoled the rumbustious berserker into the landing-net. Then intervenes another spell of *dolce far niente* until you strike the next purple patch.

The rod should be long and light, the longer the better so that you can wield it without discomfort; 17 ft. is not too long; anything under 14 ft. errs on the side of shortness. To the reel line is attached from 15 to 20 yds. of "blow line". This, for fishing in a good breeze, may be of fine plaited undressed silk, but when the wind is very light the same length of floss silk should be substituted, as it catches the gentlest zephyr much better and wafts out your dap to sport upon the ripples.

A couple of yards of gut tapered to 2X or 3X will well serve as the cast, and this terminates in a round-bend hook with a generous gape between the point and the shank. The latter should be on the short side, whipped on the gut with yellow silk. The whipping should be left unvarnished, as the baited fly is pushed up on to the whipping, and a too smooth finish is apt to allow it to slip down. Hooks vary in size from No. 5, for a single May-fly, to No. 8 or 9 when two flies are used. To bait, the point of the hook is passed through the thorax under the wings, and the fly worked along until it is over the whipping. The second fly, when, as is often the case, two are used, is baited in the same manner, and the pair ride side by side. Some advocate the practice of letting the two flies face in opposite directions, but I think the flies swim the water more naturally when facing the same way, and are more effective. Baiting a May-fly is a rather delicate operation if the lure is to retain its natural form with cocked wings. Anyhow, the boatman knows all about this and will put you wise by expert demonstration.

There is one point on which all dappers are agreed, viz. that the baits should be as fresh as possible—newly hatched and still in the sub-imago stage, when they are pale green with light legs. It is in this stage that the trout see them on the water, and it is all but useless to attempt to lure the fish with the older, darker-coloured specimens. They should be collected in the morning before going afloat, and may be kept in roomy ventilated boxes or wicker cages.

To ensure success the bellying line must be so manœuvred in relation to the strength of the wind that the dap rides jauntily on the water as to the manner born, with, theoretically, none of the gut submerged. Actually you will have occasion to congratulate yourself if you have no more than three or four inches in the water. Should the dap become water-logged, the drowned fly must be replaced with a fresh bait. The newly hatched May-flies may be collected from the sheltered sides of bushes, trees, walls, etc., on the leeward shore of the water.

Drag, the dry-fly fisher's *bête noire*, is to be avoided at all costs in dapping, and it is up to the boatman to see to this by keeping the craft drifting in the exact line of the wind.

Those anglers who yearn for something more

scientific than the simple joys of dapping, may find sweet solace while the season is on in fishing the dry fly, a practice which has enlisted many recruits during the last twenty years. The conditions which make for success are quite different from those essential to dapping. Something approaching a dead calm is desirable, or, if a gentle breeze be astir, then the sheltered bays are to be sought, and the delectable time is when the Spent Gnat is thick on the water and the trout are roaming the lough in search of it.

Time was when the West Meath loughs were considered the dapper's paradise; but sport went off to a great extent on those waters, and to-day probably Loughs Corrib, Derg and Mask are the most popular hunting-grounds. The time varies somewhat on these loughs, but normally the May-fly season occupies the latter half of May and the first half of June.

But when the last Drake has vanished the dapper's sport has by no means ended, for he substitutes the Daddy-long-legs, and small blue Dragon-fly for the May-fly, and carries on with these throughout July, August, and September. The Daddy is first choice. The insect is, at first glance, likely to strike one as but ill adapted to angling purposes, yet it is sweet to the palate of rising trout, and is little inferior to the Green Drake as a dapping bait, though more fish are missed when the Daddy is on the hook. The reason is, of course, apparent. While the May-fly is, comparatively, a convenient mouthful, the Daddy is built too much on sprawling lines to be regarded as anything in the nature of a compact morsel. Nature never made the Daddy-long-legs; she merely strung it together. It is mostly composed of a complicated problem in trigonometry, pivoted on a central exchange which does duty for a body, and is furnished with wings.

A trout feeding on Daddy-long-legs is like a man eating spaghetti—it has got to whip round the outlying suburbs of the subject before it can get all the straggling ends into its mouth. Consequently the trout, which in the first attempt only succeeds in seizing the outskirts—maybe a wing and a leg or two—of the bait is apt to be missed if the angler strikes too soon. If he pauses until the fish has taken its second grip, which usually embraces the hook, far fewer disappointments are encountered.

The same tackle is employed as in dapping with the Drake. Frequently a couple of Daddies are impaled, and in roughish water as many as three may be bunched on the hook. The flies may be collected among rough, tall grass and rushes. By disturbing these a little they will make themselves apparent, and the butterfly net does the rest.

In England dapping with the Green Drake has been practised to some extent on Derwentwater, which has a good rise of May-fly; and on the Scottish lochs blow-line fishing with the Daddy gives capital results under favourable circumstances. In his *Fifty Years with the Rod* John Stirling mentions one basket of 18 fish, weighing 18 lb., caught on Loch Awe. Loch Shiel is another water on which dapping with the Daddy has established itself.

CHAPTER XX

SHADE FISHING

SHADE fishing, *alias* dibbing, *alias* bushing, *alias* bob-bing, according to the locality in which it is practised, is virtually dapping on a less pretentious scale, and provides an occupation for the noon-tide hours of a calm, drowsy summer's day when ordinary fly fishing is temporarily out of the bill and scrambling along a rugged, rocky river-bed with the clear-water worm a weariness to the flesh.

Then the trout—many of them, and some of them big ones—are taking their siesta, or perhaps lazily cruising under the banks in the shade of the fringing trees and bushes, but with the weather eye lifting for the advent of any choice morsel that may fall from above. Or, where the river is free of arboreal frills, under the high overhanging bank. It is a stealthy, but not dextrous pastime to drop some delicate *bonne-bouche* over the neb, or in the path of the loafing fish,—something, say, big and buzzy that will effectively, but not alarmingly, invite its attention.

The fly rod of 10 ft. or so will serve admirably, and the ordinary fly line will avail in an emergency, though a fine undressed line is better, as it pays out more readily. To the reel line is attached a short cast of a couple of feet of gut; 1X is quite fine enough. This carries the hook, a round bend, which may be No. 3, 4, 5 or 6, according to the size of the bait. A foot or so above the hook is nipped on the cast a medium split shot, and threaded on the gut above this, or on the reel line, is a small perforated pistol bullet, which is prevented from slipping down to the hook by the split shot in one case, or by the knot at the end of the line in the other.

The wide choice in the variety of baits that may be used in this style of fishing is reflected in a rhyming account of "The Big Old Trout", by J. C. Dollman, which appeared in the *Graphic Summer Number* long years ago:

> And when next morn they sought the stream
>   They sank upon the ground,
> For—could it be some horrid dream?
>   The miller there they found!

> "I canna hurt your casting fly,
>   I dape wi' beetle-bug,
> Your spinner penk you still can try—
>   I dip wi' mouse or slug."

The mouse we may throw into the discard as a hopeless outsize where average trout are concerned; the slug—which is said to be most attractive when slit down the middle and turned inside out (I never tried it)—will kill at times; and the "beetle-bug", Cockroach or Cockchafer, may prove a very serviceable lure, as is also the Grasshopper.

The best of all baits, in my opinion, with which to dib is the Blue-bottle, but other large flies, such as the Green-bottle, Alder, Sedge, Wasp, Daddy-long-legs, Stone-fly and Downlooker, will serve. To bait the Blue-bottle, pass the point of the hook under the skin between the wings, so that the fly hangs from the bend beneath the hook, and, viewed from below, obscures the sight of the tackle.

Taking cover behind a convenient bush or line of

bushes, through which you can glimpse the water below, you are faced with the problem of getting rod point and bait through that interlacing network of twigs and leaves. Obviously to attempt to pass through the maze 2 ft. of dangling cast would be seeking trouble, and seeing that you get it. However, there is a simple way out of the difficulty. Reel up the line until the bullet is held against the top ring of the rod, then, holding the rod so that it points a few degrees above the horizontal, rotate it on its own axis until the dangling cast is wound snugly and spirally on the rod top.

This done, it is an easy matter, with a steady hand, to poke the outfit through the most accommodating interstice until the bait, at the other side of the bush, is over the spot it is desired to fish. But do it slowly, so that if a fish should chance to catch sight of the protrusion, it may regard it as a new shoot of merely rather rapid growth. Now the rotating of the rod in the opposite direction will unwind the cast, and the weight of the bullet draw off the paid-out line you release until the bait just touches the surface of the water, where you can allow it to buzz about and enjoy itself. By and by, if you are lucky, a trout will come along and join in the fun.

As you see it take the bait the instinct to strike at once must be sternly suppressed, otherwise that trout will miss your hook and take its own. Instead of striking immediately, ease the line a little while you count six steadily, or until the fish begins to move away, then strike, and play it as best you can, after which you will find yourself up against another problem, that of getting your prize out. To effect this a long-shafted landing-net is essential—one of 5 ft. or so, such as is used when wading as a support—and even then considerable ingenuity may be called for before the job is successfully accomplished.

In dibbing from an overhanging bank the process is much the same as that described, but you have no covering screen to hide your manly figure, and you may have to humiliate yourself to the extent of grovelling on your tummy in order to keep out of sight. Here, however, you have no difficulty in landing your fish.

Occasionally dibbing with the artificial fly, preferably a hackled or palmer pattern, is resorted to with some success, but it is not ordinarily practised. Usually the dibber is found on the banks of moorland streams and rivers, but this method of fishing will kill on the chalk streams. It is not a very artistic method, but it has the merit of ridding the water of some of the old cannibals that, reverse of the customary order of things, live on their poor relations.

As an instance of what might occur in the case of the dibbed bait being offered to the unsophisticated trout on some virgin stream, but which certainly could not happen on British waters, I succumb to the temptation of quoting here a passage from Viscount Milton and Dr Cheadle's *North-West Passage by Land*, describing their penetration, in 1863, into the then uncharted wilds of Western Canada: "On the next morning we again struck the M'Leod, and continued to follow it for a couple of days. In a small tributary we caught a few trout in a somewhat novel manner. Whilst dinner was being prepared, we went down to the stream with the boy, to fish with some of the gadflies which we caught on the horses. A number of trout were lying in the shade of a large overhanging alder, and we disposed ourselves along the trunk, in order to drop the tempting fly before the noses of the fish.

Cheadle, in his eagerness to accomplish this, fell head first into the water with a tremendous splash, and the boy, in his amusement at his companion's misfortune, slipped also, and splashed in after him. Finding that the fish immediately returned to the protecting shade, in spite of their fright, and were even then too sleepy to take the bait, we set the boy to manage the fly, while we stirred up the fish judiciously with a long pole. They were then sufficiently roused from their lethargic state to notice the bait, and a good dish of them was secured. Not one had been taken before this device was adopted."

CHAPTER XXI

OTHER BAIT FISHING

HITHERTO maggot fishing for trout has been a subject almost universally tabooed in polite angling literature; in fact, I can only recall at the moment one book, devoted exclusively to catching trout, which has mentioned it, and then only to revile it. The author of the book referred to concludes his little tilt with this paragraph: "Anyone can catch a trout fishing with a maggot, as no skill whatever is required beyond keeping out of sight. A child with five minutes' practice could easily catch trout once he has attracted the fish by the judicious application of a few maggots from time to time to the stream immediately above the pool he intends to fish."

On the other hand, no less an accredited sportsman than Major J. W. Hills, himself a devotee of the dry fly, openly confesses, in *My Sporting Life*: "I should not be baring my whole heart unless I told also of maggot fishing. To some people the idea is revolting: for me it has a great attraction. . . . It improves the trout fisher, for practice with the maggot makes him a better performer with the fly. I know it does. It gives you an inner knowledge of your water and your trout which fly fishing never affords. It is like opening a new book, the pursuit is at once simplified, and calls for a higher art. . . . It is a delicate art, and difficult. Try it."

The two authors I have quoted regard maggot fishing from two entirely different standpoints. The first, it seems from the context, in his righteous indignation at the abuses so frequently associated, alas! with the use of this bait, has lost sight of its sporting possibilities; the latter is concerned only with methods in which the objectionable practices have no part.

There is nothing illegal in maggot fishing, and the extent to which it is pursued to-day on trout waters where the rules of riparian owners or lessees do not prohibit it, would be incredible to anglers nurtured only in fly fishing circles. A little while ago I saw in a paper the statement that of the trout caught in British waters the majority were taken on the maggot. There is no means of proving, or disproving, this hazardous assertion; but I can well believe it if "certain districts" is substituted for "British waters"; for in such certain districts there are miles and miles of unrestricted trout rivers on which maggot fishing is generally practised from beginning to end of the season.

To the liberal-minded angler there can be no more objection to fishing the maggot as a hook-bait than to the same use of a worm. It is the prodigal use of ground-bait, to which the maggot fisher is often addicted, that is the bone of bitter contention between him and the fly fisher. From the ethical point of view alone ground-baiting for trout is abhorrent to the soul of the fly fisher; he places it on the same level of un-sportsmanship as throwing down a handful of corn to attract a covey of partridges, and then blazing into the brown. But, materially, there is something worse in it than that. The trout is for the most part dependent on bottom food for its sustenance, and when the feast of succulent maggots is spread before it on the river-bed—sprinkled in while fishing is in progress or shot in when the bait-bag is emptied at the end of the day

—it gorges itself on the free treat instead of having to work for its living, or a portion of it, by rising to less substantial morsels on the surface. In this way many lengths of good trout streams have been ruined for the fly fisher by wholesale ground-baiting, and he has been driven to seek his sport elsewhere. Every angler has the right of adopting what legitimate method of fishing he may fancy, but every sportsman should refrain from practices which spoil the sport for others. I remember hearing of a notice exhibited in some public gardens: "Ladies and gentlemen will not, and others must not, pluck the flowers". If it could be gently intimated to anglers that sportsmen will not, and others must not, use ground-bait for trout many of our easily accessible streams would be better places to fish in.

The method of maggot fishing indulged in by Major Hills was the *modus operandi* of the upstream worm fisher, and that only on shrunken streams. The cast should be fine, certainly no thicker than 4X, and a single crystal hook, No. 12 or 13, Redditch scale (equivalent to the fly fisher's No. 2 or 1) may be substituted for the worm tackle. It will usually be found that a couple of maggots will give the best results. To bait these the point of the hook should be inserted half-way down from the pointed end of the maggot and passed along just under the skin until it emerges at the thick end, when the other maggot is impaled by the lip of the thick end and left to dangle. Necessarily the fragile nature of the bait calls for great care in casting lest the succulent morsels—especially the one hanging on by the figurative skin of its teeth—be jerked off. The baited tackle, unshotted, is cast upstream and allowed to trickle back with the current, when the only indication of a bite is the stoppage of the line. The thin glides are also productive, but here the bait is apt to loiter in contact with the river-bed, and bites are more difficult to detect.

The common practice of the maggot fisher, however, is to swim the bait as in roach fishing, for which, although there is a growing tendency towards the use of the fixed-spool reel, the free-running Aerial probably remains first favourite. In any case it is essential in fishing long swims that provision should be present for the paying out of the line easily and evenly. The same hook, with a couple of maggots, as already described, may be employed, and for a start the float may be adjusted so that the bait swims close to the bottom. If nothing then happens, it may be that the trout are feeding on the rising nymphs in mid-water, when the float can be readjusted accordingly.

If anyone should be possessed of the notion that maggot fishing is nothing but a child's game, let him, as I have done, watch an expert at work in clear water. The delicacy of his tackle would astound the fly fisher who prides himself on fishing fine; for the cast is often of alleged 10X gut—and most certainly the finest I ever saw—terminating in a microscopic hook hidden in a single maggot. And the way in which he must, and does, deal with a lusty trout on such cobweb tackle is a revelation in the art of playing a fish.

Lest it should be thought that I am unduly biased in favour of this, to many, obnoxious form of angling, let me add that I have never fished a maggot for trout in my life, and do not suppose I ever shall. But I have seen enough of maggot fishing to appreciate its possibilities and, no less heartily, deplore the abuses which often accompany it, and without some reference to what is to-day one of the most widely practised methods of catching trout by rod and line, a book on modern trout fishing would be incomplete.

Another much-favoured bait, favoured both by the trout and the angler when it is available, is the wasp grub. First catch your grub, the preliminary to which is the locating of the wasp nest, often in a bank. The entrance is located by the ingress and egress of the yellow-jackets, the spifflication of which is the first part of the programme. The modern method of effecting this is with the aid of cyanide of potassium, otherwise prussic acid, and the time for its application is in the evening when all the wasps have come home and are safe indoors. A thin roll of blotting-paper, about the diameter of the little finger, should be pushed part-way into the hole and a good dose of the cyanide poured on it; or the cyanide may be simply poured on the entrance. In either case the massacre is speedily assured.

Of course, prussic acid is a deadly poison and should not be left lying about. To avoid all risks of a coroner's inquest, many prefer to adopt the old-fashioned process of preparing a squib by kneading up damp gunpowder into a solid cylinder about the thickness of the finger and 5 or 6 in. in length. This is poked, lighted, into the hole, which is then promptly tamped with a sod. After the lapse of a few minutes the nest may be dug out.

The wasp grubs may be fished with float tackle after the manner of maggots, though it is advisable to use a rather larger hook, say a No. 9, and a couple, or even three, make a presentable dose. Unfortunately, while the trout, it is strongly suspected, prefer to take the dainty *au naturel*, the bait in that condition is difficult to keep on the hook, and it is customary to toughen it by baking or steaming. In the former procedure the layers of comb are placed in a slow oven and kept under observation so that they can be removed before

Shade Fishing

MAGGOT FISHING

the grubs get too hard. Steaming is effected by placing the comb in an earthen jar, which in turn is placed in a pan with sufficient water in it to produce the steam, but not to bubble over into the jar. Cover the whole and simmer.

The Caddis grub, or Cad-bait, is another toothsome morsel for which the trout often display a marked predilection in the summer months. It is, of course, the larva of one or other of the *Trichoptera*, which may be found crawling about the bed of the shallow streams or pools, their head and legs protruding from the wonderful cylindrical suits of clothes they have fashioned out of tiny pebbles, sticks or straws, and which they trail about with them, the abdominal portions of their persons still concealed within. These may be collected, and kept, in their cases for a few days in a ventilated tobacco-tin in which is placed a little damp moss. They can be fished with float tackle in the same way as the maggots; or, as some bait fishers prefer, the float may be omitted and they can be fished in the deepish pools and slacks on very fine shotted tackle with a sink-and-draw motion, somewhat in the manner of the drop-minnow described in a previous chapter.

Another larval *bonne-bouche* which appeals to the trout's epicurean palate is the dock- or docken-grub. This is the yellowish-white caterpillar of the ghost moth, the "bustard" of the north, and is found about the roots of the dock and a few other plants on which it feeds. It is about two inches in length and, on worm tackle, it may be substituted for the worm in clear-water upstream fishing; still on the worm tackle and shotted, it can be "swum" with a float.

CHAPTER XXII

THAMES TROUTING

In some respects, and to some degree, it might be said that the *éclat* has departed from Thames trout fishing. It may be that the introduction of tens of thousands of imported fish has so greatly increased the number of trout in the river that the capture of a specimen is not now the sensational event in an angler's life it once was when that capture was the crowning glory of weeks, sometimes months, of persistent effort and observation.

The length of the protracted campaign was, no doubt, responsible for the story of the visitor who, after watching an angler assiduously spinning a bleak over one of the Thames weir-pools for a very long time with, apparently, no result, at last ventured to approach him and inquire:

"Fishing for Thames trout?"

"Yes."

"Has—er—any been caught here lately?"

"Dunno, guv'nor," was the reply; "this is only the second season I been here."

Or it may be that, while a generation or so ago the Thames trout was, practically, the only game fish within easy access of the resident in the Thames Valley, improved methods of rapid transport have lead him further afield in search of more easily attainable thrills. Probably Thames trouting was at the peak of its fame in the minds of the devout—and there

were Thames-trouting "fans" a-plenty in those days—
during the closing years of last century, when, it has
been observed, the sport worked out something like
this: The whole of the first year of your novitiate you
occupied in endeavouring to spot a fish. This you
might do, if you were very lucky, about the end of the
season when it was too late to fish for it. You devoted
the second year to observing the habits of the fish you
had spotted, particularly noting the times at which it
fed and when it took its afternoon nap, and to studying
the currents and taking the temperature of the water.
The third season, making use of the knowledge you
had accumulated the previous year, you fished in-
dustriously for the fish you had spotted. The fourth
year somebody else caught it, which left you free
to set about spotting another one and commencing
de novo.

An exaggeration, of course, but it had some flimsy
foundation of fact. Use the pruning knife judiciously,
and compare it with the facts actually surrounding the
capture of what is usually claimed as the record
Thames trout, as narrated by Jock Scott in his *Game
Fish Records*: "The story of its capture is an amusing
one. . . . The captor was a Mr Wicks, a professional
fisherman, and the date 1880.

"Now Wicks had a client who knew all about this
fish, and had, in fact, tried for it on many occasions.
Like most big trout, it kept to its own preserve, and
fed at more or less regular hours.

"On the fateful day Wicks had received notice of his
client's arrival and was on hand with the necessary
tackle and so on. Time passed, and the client did not
arrive; but the fish began to feed. One can imagine
Wicks' feelings; there was the monster feeding in full
view, everything ready—and no client! The tempta-

tion was irresistible! Wicks made a cast or two, the fish was hooked and eventually killed.

"Great was the wrath of the client; and it is hardly necessary to add that he found another professional fisherman: Wicks thus achieving fame at the expense of his pocket."

In those days Thames trouting was not only a thing apart from other trout fishing; it wore a halo, and was only to be pursued with long and earnest effort. Mr F. H. Amphlett, the veteran authority on Thames fishing, related some time ago, in the *Shooting Times*, how a Hampton Court professional fisherman once went up to Tagg's Hotel and asked a gentleman staying there if he would like to go trout fishing.

"Are there any trout in the water?" asked the visitor.

"Oh yes, plenty," replied the professional.

"Well," said the gentleman, "I don't care about going fishing myself, but you might catch me a brace for breakfast."

It is not recorded what immediately followed this sacrilegious suggestion or whether the professional Thames fisherman ever fully recovered from the shock.

Since those days the lustre of the halo has dimmed a little, owing to the fact that the capture of a specimen of 10 lb. or upwards is a very rare occurrence. The fish caught by Wicks weighed 16 lb. 15 oz.; but it seems it was not taken actually in the Thames, but in the Kennet, a tributary. There are, however, more or less vague reports of the Thames having yielded still larger trout, concerning which *The Field*'s publication, *Where to Fish*, stated: "A Thames fish of 17¼ lb. was caught in a net below Isleworth a good many years ago and returned to the river alive. A fish of 17 lb. 3 oz. was reported caught near Radcot Bridge about

1899, but the data were obscure. A 22-pounder is said to have been caught at Windsor about 1834, by Gen. Sir Samuel Hawker, and to have been sent by him to the King."

There are several records of specimens of 12 to 14 lb. having been taken in those spacious days; now the angler is extraordinarily lucky to land one over 6 lb. Still, the increase in numbers compensates to some extent for the decline in individual bulk. It is very doubtful if any of the original Thames breed still survives; but that is no great matter, seeing that the newcomers, such is the influence of diet and environment, take on the appearance and characteristics of the aborigines.

Nor is there anything really remarkable about the Thames trout attaining to the great size they do. It is the rule that obtains in water infested with predatory coarse fish, as is the Thames. These piscine pirates take heavy toll of the trout fry, but such of the latter as are lucky enough to escape the jaws of the buccaneers, themselves, on reaching maturity, retaliate by gorging on the smaller coarse fish, and on the bountiful banquets of minnows and bleak, with which the Thames abounds, plump themselves out to noble proportions.

The most sporting, and most difficult, method of Thames trouting is spinning. An artificial spinner, Phantom or Devon, may be used, but by far the best bait is a small bleak or dace. A popular form of spinning flight used on the Thames consists of a lip-hook and a series of four triangles. The lip-hook is, of course, passed through the lips of the bait, and the four triangles held in place by inserting one hook of each in the side of the bleak, the fourth triangle, inserted just below the tail, is so arranged that that part of the

bait's anatomy is curved to give it a spin. And the bait
must spin—not wobble. Much of its success depends on
its ability, directed by competent hands, to commence
a brilliant rotation the moment it touches the water.
Should the angler lack skill in mounting the bait so as
to produce a straight spin with the curved fish, then
let him resort to the use of one of the many excellent
tackles on the market which produce the desired effect
of a scintillating streak through the water with the aid
of a pair of small metal fans, the fans being chromium-
plated for preference.

A moderately fine link of undrawn gut may be used
next to the tackle; above this 4 or 5 ft. of rather stouter
gut will serve as a trace, and on this trace should be
fixed an "anti-kink" lead, small for the quieter streams,
and larger for the heavy waters of the weirpools. The
size of the lead should be determined by its capacity
for keeping the bait working a good foot below the
surface. A double swivel should be inserted below the
lead. The reel line may well be of dressed plaited silk,
as fine as may be compatible with the size of the
quarry.

The method of spinning for Thames trout is pretty
much the same as that employed in spinning for pike;
but the man accustomed to pike fishing must accelerate
the pace of his bait from a deliberate revolution to
a dizzy flashing round that commences as contact is
made with the water.

At the beginning of the season it is not easy to know
which are the best places over which to spin, as the
fish are then more or less scattered, many of them in
the quieter waters; but as the season advances, even if
no particular fish has been spotted, it is always worth
while to fish the weirpool "on spec." Best of all is it to
put oneself in the hands of a professional fisherman,

who knows the favourite haunts of the quarry and is ever on the lookout to make note of the whereabouts of the trout and their usual meal-times for the benefit of his clients. He may also be looked to for the supply of bait and tackle.

However, while spinning is by far the more artistic and sporting way of fishing for Thames trout, the more popular, and easier, method is live-baiting, though in this case success is largely dependent on knowing where a fish is feeding, or where one is likely to be. The bleak is the bait usually pressed into service, and the customary tackle consists of a triangle attached to the end of the gut, and a small lip-hook tied on above it, the distance between the two being regulated so that when the lip-hook is put through the upper lip of the bleak one point of the triangle may conveniently be fixed under the skin by the back fin. The gut, reasonably fine but strong, need not be more than 2 yds. in length, and 1 yd. or so above the bait the line is buoyed with a small cork float. A little round affair, such as is used in swimming the worm, described in another chapter, or the "pilot" float of the pike fisher will serve; but, to subscribe to the ancient orthodox faith, the correct thing is a small medicine-bottle cork, which may be cut half-way through and the gut jammed in the slit. A light reel line, well-greased and plenty of it—for the fight may be a duel at long range—is desirable.

Mooring the punt 20, 30 or even 40 yds. above the spot where the trout is feeding—or ought to be feeding —the bait is drifted down to it, allowed to play about there, and the subsequent proceedings are in the lap of the gods. Should a lively 5- or 6-pounder annex the bleak for keeps, a hectic five minutes is likely to ensue.

Fly fishing for Thames trout is not a profitable

pursuit, and is little practised. Still, it is possible, especially in the tumbled waters of a weirpool, to catch them on loch or grilse flies, or large Sedges, or, most likely of all, on the Alexandra. It is usually the small Thames trout of under 1 lb. in weight which succumb to such allurements, yet there are very rare exceptions, and Jock Scott, in *Game Fish Records*, cites as the record Thames trout caught on fly one of 8 lb. killed in Marlow weirpool by Dr Shone, and, as the runner-up, another of 7 lb. caught by Mr Clare Sturges on a Coachman when fishing for chub.

CHAPTER XXIII

SEA TROUT FISHING

The sea trout is possessed of more names than a Spanish grandee of ancient lineage; indeed, it is known, mostly locally, by upwards of fourscore appellations, and these are exclusive of what the angler calls it in inspired moments of exasperation.

Adorning this bewildering multitude of designations we find such picturesque specimens as red-fin, yellow-fin, salmon-pink, black-neb, blue-cap, blue-fin, graellaspring, finnock, herling, herring-sprod, Lammas-man, sprat, moudie-trout, rack-rider, scad, skagger, brith-dail, Candlemas-grey, silver-grey, fork-tail, cockivie, gwiniad, mort, peal, pug, round-tail, twb-y-dail, salmon-scurf, etc. etc. To avoid confusion, the Salmon and Freshwater Fisheries Act of 1923 lumps the lot under the head of "migratory trout", meaning "trout which migrate to and from the sea".

Still, the more commonly known of the unscientific names have a certain useful significance for the angler. Thus, the young sea trout at the time of its first migration to the sea is generally recognised as a smolt. Whitling, finnock and herling are terms applied to the same fish after it reaches the sea and until its mature return to freshwater, a period which includes the summer, autumn and winter following the smolt stage. The second summer sees the sea trout's arrival at the adult stage, whereupon, according to locality, it is known variously as a mort, peal, sewin or white trout, the last being the usual name for sea trout in Ireland. Incidentally the sea trout, like the salmon, from the fry stage to that of the smolt is called a parr.

Formerly the sea trout was regarded as a distinct species and many works on trout fishing completely ignored it, but, as I have previously said, ichthyologists are now generally agreed that there is but one species of trout in the British Isles. Of this species the sea trout is one form that has developed, or retained, as the case may be, the sea-going habit. Formerly, too —indeed, up to quite recent years—it was held that the sea trout was no deep sea rover, never venturing far from the mouth of the river that gave it birth; but later investigation has disproved this. Summing up the general results of extensive markings of fish, W. J. M. Menzies states in his *Sea Trout and Trout* (1936): "First of all, it is quite clear that the older idea that sea trout cling close to their river of origin was founded on insufficient evidence and in the light of modern research is no longer tenable. They are capable of performing really long journeys up to at least four hundred miles in length and most probably go for a considerable distance, say up to one and possibly two hundred miles, in their normal migrations in search of food."

There is a curious point about the return of sea trout to the freshwater which, to my mind, has never been satisfactorily explained: Among the shoals of fish invading the rivers are vast numbers of immature whitling which do not spawn, and, therefore, it seems to be almost beyond the bounds of possibility that the early return of these young non-spawners is actuated by the propagatory instinct, although it must be admitted that a small percentage of the whitling are precocious specimens which do ripen in the first year of their post-smolt life and do spawn on their first return to their native haunts. It is suggested as a possible explanation that, the sea trout being gregarious in its habits, the run of non-spawners with the spawners is a matter of mere herding instinct. If that be so, it must be a powerful instinct that will tempt vigorous young appetites away from the marine flesh-pots to the comparatively scant larder of the river.

Apparently the movements of the whitling are complicated. It would seem that, descending to the sea in April or May, some of them reappear in freshwater in the following July, indulging in backward and forward manœuvres, while others remain in the salt water until they arrive at the adult stage in the following year, running early or late according to the rivers of their origin. Usually the most numerous runs occur in August, and may continue in decreasing numbers through September into October, more or less simultaneously with the runs of older fish, so that sea-trout fishing constitutes itself a summer sport, to be pursued, often with thrilling results, in river, loch, and voe. For the silvery sea trout, once hooked, is full of dash and devilment, an acrobatic diehard that keeps the angler in a quiver of excited suspense from its first glittering meteoric flash into the air to the moment when it is drawn over the landing-net.

The whitling after their first year of sea life may run from ½ to ¾ lb., after which the sea trout is roughly estimated to gain a pound in weight for each year of sea life, and may attain to the heavy-weight class, the average varying considerably in different districts. Thus, in some waters the usual weight may run from 1 to 2 lb., in others 3- and 4-pounders may be fairly common, and occasionally fish of brobdingnagian proportions are landed. The largest rod-caught sea trout on record was one of 28 lb. caught on the river Em, in Sweden, by W. H. Barrett, in 1930, and, singularly, the second heaviest was landed by the same angler in the previous year. It weighed 26½ lb. England's sea trout record stands at 21 lb. with a fish from the Frome. Wales has yielded to the angler one fish of 20 lb. 2 oz. and a few 16- and 17-pounders; while Scotland's best was one of 16 lb. landed on the Ailort, one of the few rivers which has a good run of spring sea trout. (*See note on page* 198.)

The sea trout is an accommodating quarry insomuch as it may be caught by any of the numerous methods usually employed for the capture of brown trout, though to obtain the best results the strength of the tackle, the size of the lures, and even the fashion of using them are somewhat modified. Most frequently the artificial fly is used, occasionally fished dry but more often wet. Next in popular favour comes the worm, fished pretty much as for brown trout in thick and clear water respectively, which accounts for heavy baskets in a blinding flood. The minnow, natural or artificial, is also utilised with killing effect under somewhat similar conditions. Even dapping with the natural insect, as practised with the May-fly for brown trout, and in the manner I have already described, annually kills its thousands of sea trout, though, of course, the May-fly season is over before the sea trout run in numbers, and for presentation to the latter fish the Daddy-long-legs is the favourite *bonne-bouche*.

The idyllic way of offering the dap is from a boat on a lake, as it is popularly practised on Loch Shiel; but the bait is in skilful hands often a fatal lure on the rivers. Here the difficulties in approaching the fish are much greater, as, if angling from the bank, the pool can only be fished from the windward shore, and the breeze on a tree-sheltered stream is much more fitful than on the

open loch, which may call for almost constant lengthening or shortening of the line. In the gentlest of zephyrs
a fluffy feather tied on the end of the blow-line next to
the gut will sometimes act as a sort of aerial float
to prevent the line from drowning, while, in a strong
breeze, a small shot nipped on the gut an inch or two
above the dap will have a restraining effect upon its
vaulting ambition to fly sky-high.

As I have said, it is often expedient in fishing for sea
trout to employ modifications of the methods which
would be most suitable for brown trout fishing. Thus
it is usual to use stronger tackle, not merely because
the sea trout is a more robust fighter and may run to
twice the size of the brownie in the same water, but
also because sea trout water is likewise salmon water,
and there is always a fair sporting chance that *Salar*
may take your fly or lure at any moment, when, if fine
tackle were employed, a speedy smash would be the
result in nine cases out of ten.

In recent years anglers have shown a tendency
towards refinement in the size of gut used in sea trout
fishing, and the necessity for using the coarse stuff to
which our grandfathers were partial is falling into disrepute. I think I should not be far wrong in stating
that the generality of fly fishers would now regard 1X
or finest undrawn as the minimum for loch fishing and
night fishing on the rivers, though a minority of day
fishers on the rivers use 2X and 3X, and dry-fly fishers
will sometimes pin their faith to 4X.

Moving in shoals and shifting their haunts with the
fluctuating height of water in the river, it is not always
easy for the angler to determine the whereabouts of the
fish, unless he is possessed of a fair amount of river lore
and is intimately acquainted with the stream. But it
may be taken that the sea trout love comfortable lies

calling for the expenditure of a minimum amount of exertion in maintaining their positions. Thus, the rough water that may yield a brace or two of brown trout will probably be barren of their roving brothers; although a fairly fast boulder-strewn stream will often hold sea trout—not in the fast currents but in the eddying pockets before or behind the boulders. The shallowing tail of a pool is frequently a favourite haunt.

On the Scottish waters sea trout rods of 13 or 14 ft. are common objects of the loch or riverside, but as one works southward he finds an increasing disposition to make the ordinary stiffish 10- or 10½-footer serve. For wet-fly fishing in the rivers during the day three flies may be mounted, but for night angling no more than two are advisable, and these should be 3 or 4 ft. apart. For dry-fly work one fly only is, of course, used. Nine feet is a convenient length for the cast.

Occasionally one comes across a sturdy advocate of upstream fishing with the wet fly on the sea trout rivers, but the common practice is to fish the cast across and down, allowing the current to carry the flies along with as little let or hindrance as may be practicable until they hang in the stream below. Occasionally, too, one encounters the man who devoutly believes in working his flies as in salmon fishing, but to my way of thinking there is little, if any, advantage to be gained thereby. I do think, however, that it is good medicine to allow the cast to hang in the stream for a few moments— even to give it a little tempting draw or two before picking up the line for a fresh throw. It always reminds me of the auctioneer's "Now, gentlemen, this is positively your last chance! One! two! three!" before the lot on offer is withdrawn. For a fish may have followed the fly for some distance with a half-hearted hesitancy that may thus be overcome at the last moment. At times the sea trout will best take the fly well sunk, in which case the angler should endeavour to get his cast submerged as quickly as possible after it touches the water. At other times the fly fished near the surface seems the more attractive. There is no fixed rule; the sea trout's moods are tantalisingly difficult to gauge, and it is only by experiment that the best course to pursue is discoverable.

Dry-fly fishing for sea trout is the sport of the minority, practised on calm, clear and often low water, and small flies and fine gut—say 4X—give the best results. When there is a hatch of the natural flies, and fish are seen rising to them, a passable imitation of the fly being taken is, of course, the particular tempter to use; but these conditions are the exception, and ordinarily the sacred tenets of the exact imitation and fishing the rise only go by the board and, selecting what he considers the likeliest fly, the angler proceeds to put it over what he considers the likeliest spots.

However, there are many days when—especially in the low clear water that is a common feature of the summer rivers—fly fishing, either wet or dry, is well-nigh hopeless so long as daylight remains, and the angler must needs resort to night fishing to compensate him for the earlier barren hours. Indeed, the sea trout generally is much easier to catch after the shades of evening fall, and it is then that it is mostly fished for on the majority of our rivers. Many anglers prefer a dark night, though moonlight by no means rules out the chance of sport.

Rod and tackle may be those used with the wet fly during the daytime, but no more than two flies should be mounted on the cast. The surroundings are those of the Bustard fisher already described, and the scene of action is, for choice, the shallow tail of a pool known to be haunted by the quarry. The cast is varied, up-stream, downstream, and across in the process of searching the water thoroughly, and the line is drawn in after the flies have made their entry in the water. Once the shoal of fish is located there is little need to shift one's ground. A pocket torch is a great convenience when it comes to changing a cast or unhooking a fish.

Fly fishing for sea trout on a loch differs in no material instance from the method described in the chapter on "Lake Fishing" as to the manner of manipulating one's gear, but the whereabouts of the fish are more difficult to discover. On the great lakes, like the Scottish lochs and the Irish loughs, the visiting angler, left to his own resources, might easily waste the whole of his holiday in a futile search. The assistance of a reliable boatman who knows the hidden features of the water and the spots most favoured as resting-places by the shoals is the only assurance of success.

Of the wet flies used in sea trout fishing the great majority are large fancy patterns that might be classed as small salmon flies, in fact, several of the orthodox salmon patterns, dressed small, are regularly pressed into service. The following will be found among the most popular sea trout flies: Black Zulu, Blue Zulu, Blae and Black, Blae and Blue, Butcher, Bloody Butcher, Connemara Black, Dunkeld, Grouse and Claret, Hen Pheasant and Yellow, Mallard and Claret (the most popular of all), Peter Ross (another special favourite) and Silver Doctor. The sizes of hooks vary according to conditions and waters. There is no hard and fast rule governing them. Nos. 6 and 7 (New Scale) are common sizes, with something smaller, say No. 2 or 3, for low water. The dressings of the flies in the above list will be found in Chapter XXIV.

SEA TROUT FISHING IN CONNEMARA

It would be difficult, if not impossible, to say what are the most popular patterns for dry-fly work. Many of the well-known trout patterns, dressed large, are used according to the taste and fancy of the user. Special dry-fly sea trout patterns I do not know, except that in his *Sea Trout and Other Fishing Studies* Dr J. C. Mottram gives two dressings he has evolved out of his observation and experience:

"Black Variant. Body, black ostrich herl; wings, short brown fibres from the tail of the English partridge tied in on either side like the points of a camel hair brush; two or three turns of black ostrich herl in front of the wings; hackle, long glossy black continued down the body.

"Red Gnat. Body, unstripped condor quill; wings, the tip of a secondary feather from the wing of a thrush or sparrow, tied in horizontally over the body; in front of the wing two or three turns of black ostrich herl; hackle, glossy, red, rather long, not continued down the body but placed in front of the horizontal wing."

By far most of the bait fishing for sea trout is done—perhaps some of my readers would prefer the word "perpetrated"—in the thick coloured waters of a blinding flood with the assistance of the lowly lob. This is a very killing method, to compensate for which the peak of hectic opportunity is usually of short duration, as sea trout rivers are prone to wax rapidly and to be almost as quick to wane. Worming for sea trout differs little from worming for brown trout, though the tackle may be stronger.

Either the single hook, Pennell tackle or Stewart tackle is utilised, and a lobworm of 6 or 7 in. is a likely bait for thick water. Failing a wriggler of this size, a couple of 3 or 4 in. may be substituted. The important point is to shot the tackle so that the bait trundles unsuspiciously along the bottom of the stream, and that is pretty nearly all there is to it. In heavy water the sea trout may hug the sides of the flood, or they may be spread abroad in a wide stretch where the current is less concentrated. Therefore, operations should be extended over the water within reach.

In clear water the tactics of the upstream wormer are adopted, and occasionally a few good fish may be picked up by casting a long line down and across, and, so to speak, drifting the bait down to where a shoal has been spotted.

It is when the water is clearing after a spate, but has not yet fined down to a fly water, that the spinner may look for his best baskets, though he may, with the exercise of a moderate degree of skill, continue to score until the river has run in to normal height and clarity. The natural bait is the most killing, and the minnow is probably the most favoured lure, though there are many Scottish sea trout fishers who stoutly acclaim the loach as second to none. Of artificial spinners the Devon is as good as any.

On the Scottish sea lochs, kyles, and voes sea trout fishing is energetically pursued with substantial reward in the shape of heavy baskets. Sometimes the fly is fished with a fair amount of success, but the surest aids to a weighty creel are the black-headed lobworm and the sand eel. The former is cast and fished with a sink-and-draw motion, while the latter is baited on spinning tackle.

NOTE

Two of the sea-trout records quoted on page 192 have been surpassed. The English record, also from the Dorset Frome, stands at 22½ lb., and the Scottish, from the Awe, at 21 lb. At least one other 20-pounder has been landed from the Dovey in Wales, and in Scotland the Ythan has yielded one of 18 lb. 2 oz. and the Moidart one of 19 lb. 12 oz.

CHAPTER XXIV

FAMILIAR TROUT FLIES AND THEIR DRESSINGS

THE number of patterns of artificial trout flies is legion, and in many instances one may come across a score or more of dressings for a single pattern, so that to attempt here anything like a comprehensive list is out of the question. I confine myself to familiar flies which have been mentioned in the preceding pages, taking them alphabetically.

ALDER

Body.—Bronze peacock harl, ribbed with waxed claret silk.
Wings.—Speckled brown hen's wing feather.
Hackle.—Black cock.

The above is a good dry-fly pattern. For wet-fly fishing a brown speckled grouse hackle is substituted.

ALEXANDRA

Body.—Flat silver tinsel.
Wings.—Bright green peacock harl, with a strand of red ibis up each side.
Hackle.—Black hen.
Tail.—Red ibis.

This is a useful sea trout fly, and is probably taken by the fish for some *recherché* brand of minnow. In a former generation, and as a brown trout fly, it had such an evil reputation as a wholesale slaughterer that its use was rigidly barred on many waters, where it was regarded as something akin, in its effects, to salmon roe. Actually it never fully deserved the maledictions that were showered upon it, and to-day, I think, it is generally recognised that, while at times it may prove a useful lure, it is by no means an epidemic of sudden death.

BLACK GNAT (Halford's Dressing)

Body.—Undyed peacock quill, with a few turns of brown horsehair at the shoulder.
Wings.—Pale dun hackle points.
Hackle.—Starling's glossy black neck feather.
Head.—Three turns pale maroon horsehair.

BLACK GNAT (Skues's Dressing, as given in *Minor Tactics of the Chalk Stream*)

Body.—Black tying silk with two turns of black ostrich harl or knob of black silk at the shoulder.
Wings.—Palest snipe rolled and reversed.
Legs.—Black hen, or cock starling's crest, two turns at most.

Above two patterns were evolved with special reference to the Hampshire chalk streams. The following will be found a good, and simple, pattern for the wet fly:

Body.—Black horsehair for choice, otherwise black tying silk.
Hackle.—Glossy black neck feather from a starling.

BLACK PALMER

Body.—Peacock harl, ribbed with flat gold tinsel.
Hackle.—Black cock, run down from shoulder to tail.

The Palmers are generally supposed to represent hairy caterpillars that fall into the river. It is also hazarded that the trout take them for some aquatic creatures.

BLACK SPIDER

Body.—Tawny brown tying silk, waxed.
Hackle.—Black feather of a starling.

This fly, very lightly dressed, was one of the favourites of W. C. Stewart, with which he killed his thousands on the Border rivers.

BLACK ZULU

Body.—Black wool, ribbed with flat silver tinsel.
Hackle.—Black cock or hen.
Tail.—Red wool or ibis feather.

A capital sea trout fly on a dark day and a popular favourite.

BLAE AND BLACK

Body.—Black floss silk or seal's fur, ribbed with silver tinsel.
Wings.—Dark wing feather from a wild duck.
Hackle.—Black hen.
Tail.—Scarlet ibis.

Dressed small this is a popular Scottish brown trout pattern; larger, it is very effective in sea trout fishing. "Blae" is the Scottish rendering of the Yorkshire "Bloa", which signifies the colour of the louring clouds of a threatening sky.

BLAE AND BLUE

Body.—Flat silver tinsel.
Wings.—Dark wing feather of a wild duck.

Hackle.—Feather dyed light blue.
Tail.—Scarlet ibis.

BLAE AND SILVER

Body.—Flat silver tinsel.
Wings.—Dark wing feather of a wild duck.
Hackle.—Pale badger.
Tail.—Scarlet ibis.

All the Blae flies are good killers in lake fishing both for brown trout and sea trout.

BLOODY BUTCHER

Body.—Flat silver tinsel.
Wings.—Dark feather from a wild duck's wing.
Hackle.—Dyed crimson feather.
Tail.—Scarlet ibis.

BLUE DUN (old North Country Dressing)

Body.—Light olive silk, waxed and partly untwined to show in light and dark ribs when wound on the hook.
Wings.—Quill feather of a starling stained in onion dye.
Hackle.—Olive dyed.
Tail.—Two rabbit's whiskers.

The Blue Dun is the same as the Early Olive Dun, of which the Waterhen Bloa is a hackled representation usually fished in the Northern Counties when the natural fly is on the water, and even in the early months of the season when there is no rise in evidence.

BLUE DUN (Dry Fly)

Body.—Light olive silk, waxed and ribbed with gold wire.

Wings.—Starling's dark wing feather.
Hackle.—Cock, dyed olive.
Tail.—Rabbit's whisks.

When the natural Blue Dun is on the water the trout will usually take a Greenwell's Glory. Though the latter is commonly regarded as a fancy fly, I have a notion that they take it for some sort of a glorified Blue Dun.

BLUE QUILL

Body.—Undyed quill of peacock's eye feather.
Wings.—Starling's wing feather.
Hackle.—Medium dun cock.
Tail.—Whisks as hackle.

For the hackled pattern omit the wings and give an extra turn of hackle.

BLUE UPRIGHT

Body.—Light peacock quill.
Hackle.—Blue dun cock.
Tail.—Three fibres of hackle.

A favourite West of England hackled form of the Blue Dun, most extensively used in Devon and Cornwall.

BLUE-WINGED OLIVE (Halford's Dressing)

Body.—Peacock quill dyed pale olive.
Wings.—Pale coot.
Hackle.—Dyed pale olive.

There are tyings galore of this popular South Country fly. Fished wet on the North Country rivers, the Poult Bloa is probably taken for the "B.W.O.".

BLUE ZULU

Body.—Black wool, ribbed with flat silver tinsel.
Hackle.—Dyed bright blue.
Tail.—Red wool or scarlet ibis.

BROWN OWL

Body.—Orange silk, waxed.
Hackle.—Ruddy brown feather from a brown owl's wing.
Head.—A turn of bronze peacock harl.

One of the imitations of the Willow Fly or Needle, popular on North Country rivers.

BUMBLE, FURNACE

Body.—Flat gold tinsel.
Hackle.—Furnace cock, run from shoulder to tail.

"Furnace" is a term for a red hackle with a black centre.

BUMBLE, HONEY DUN

Body.—Orange- or salmon-coloured floss silk, ribbed with a strand of green peacock harl.
Hackle.—Honey dun hen, run from shoulder to tail.

This is the most famous of the Derbyshire bumbles and is an old-established favourite.

BUMBLE, MULBERRY

Body.—Claret floss silk, ribbed with peacock harl.
Hackle.—Blue dun cock, run from shoulder to tail.
Known also as the Claret Bumble.

BUMBLE, YELLOW

Body.—Yellow floss silk, ribbed with a strand of bronze peacock harl.
Hackle.—Blue cock, run from shoulder to tail.

BUSTARD

Dressings for Bustards will be found in the chapter on Bustard Fishing.

BUTCHER

Body.—Flat silver tinsel.
Wings.—Dark feather from a wild duck's wing.
Hackle.—Black hen.
Tail.—Scarlet ibis.

The Butcher is a first-class all-round wet fly, and is responsible to a material extent for keeping up the troutorial death-rate to a high figure in river and lake. For loch and sea trout fishing it is one of the "indispensables", and, though none but the wildly imaginative could detect in it any semblance to the nymph, it will, and does, despite the severe disapproval of the disciplinarian, kill even South Country trout when they are nymphing.

COACHMAN

Body.—Bronze peacock harl.
Wings.—White duck.
Hackle.—Ginger cock.

Fished wet or dry, this kills best in the evening, when it is possibly taken for a moth. Dressed large it will kill when bustard fishing. Legend awards the honour of its invention to a certain royal coachman. Personally,

I always see in its white wings some suggestion of the white greatcoat of the Victorian "whip".

CINNAMON SEDGE
See SEDGES.

COCH-Y-BONDDU
Body.—Bronze peacock harl, tipped with gold tinsel.
Hackle.—Furnace cock.

The name suggests a Welsh origin, and the fly, representing a flying beetle which makes its appearance in June, is eagerly taken by the trout. A North Country imitation of the same beetle is known as the Bracken Clock.

CONNEMARA BLACK
Body.—Black wool or seal's fur, sometimes ribbed with fine silver tinsel.
Wings.—Brown feather of a mallard.
Hackle.—Blue feather from a jay's wing.
Tail.—Golden pheasant's crest feather.

One of the most popular patterns on the Irish loughs.

DARK NEEDLE
Body.—Waxed orange silk.
Hackle.—Darkest feather from a brown owl's wing, or a dark brownish shoulder feather from a starling's wing. Yorkshire pattern, imitating one of the small *Perlidæ* and good in the latter part of the season.

DARK OLIVE QUILL
See OLIVE QUILL.

DARK SNIPE AND PURPLE
Body.—Dark purple silk, well waxed.

Hackle.—A feather from the outside of a jack snipe's wing.

One of the most familiar artificials on the North Country trout fisher's list. It is popularly supposed to represent the Iron Blue Dun, but it is not a close imitation of the insect, and alternative guesses are made as to the identity of the natural it is taken for. What matters most is that the trout *do* take it readily, most readily during the early part of the season and again during the closing weeks.

DARK VARIANT

Body.—Dark quill from stem of peacock tail feather.
Wings.—Dark starling.
Hackle.—Tip of a dark grizzled blue cock hackle.

The Variants are a type of fly invented by the late Dr William Baigent, of Northallerton. They are lightly dressed with long hackles, and have become widely popular. The tying quoted is from Woolley's *Modern Trout Fly Dressing*.

DARK WATCHETT

Body.—Orange and purple silk, twisted together and dubbed sparingly with mole's fur, wrapped on the hook to show in alternate cross stripes.
Hackle.—Smoky blue feather from a jackdaw's neck.

This is a hackled form of the Iron Blue Dun. Why it is called a "Watchett" I do not know, seeing that the dictionary definition of the word is "light blue", while this fly is very dark blue. To make confusion worse confounded, an old North Country term for the Orange Partridge, in which there is no blue, is "Brown Watchett".

DUNKELD

Body.—Gold tinsel, ribbed with gold wire.
Wings.—Dark mallard with jungle cock at each side.
Hackle.—Dyed orange, run from shoulder to tail.
Tail.—Golden pheasant's crest feather.

GINGER QUILL

Body.—Light undyed peacock quill.
Wings.—Pale starling from the wing.
Hackle.—Ginger cock.
Tail.—Three fibres of hackle.

GOLD-RIBBED HARE'S EAR

Body.—Fur from the base of a hare's ear, spun on yellow silk and ribbed with flat gold tinsel.
Wings.—Pale starling from the wing.
Hackle.—Long fibres of the hare's fur.
Tail.—Three fibres of hackle.

Originally a South Country pattern, the virtues of this fly are now known everywhere.

GOVERNOR

Body.—Bronze peacock harl, with a primrose floss tip.
Wings.—Woodcock wing feather.
Hackle.—Ginger cock.

GRANNOM (Ronalds's Pattern)

Body.—Fur of hare's face left rough, spun on brown silk. A little green floss silk may be worked in at the tail to represent the bunch of eggs there.
Wings.—Feather from the partridge's wing, and made very full.
Hackle.—Pale ginger hen.

Although Ronalds published this dressing a hundred years ago it is still a very useful pattern.

GREENWELL'S GLORY

Body.—Yellow tying silk, waxed with cobbler's wax, to impart to the body a greenish-yellow hue. This is ribbed over with yellow gimp or finest gold wire.
Wings.—Blackbird, tied in a bunch and split.
Hackle.—Coch-y-bonddu.

Many variations are published of the dressing of this famous fly. The one given here is that given to E. M. Tod by Canon Greenwell himself, and published in Tod's *Wet-fly Fishing*.

GROUSE AND CLARET

Body.—Claret seal's fur, ribbed with gold wire.
Wings.—Feather from the wing or tail of a grouse.
Hackle.—Dyed claret.
Tail.—Golden pheasant tippet.

GROUSE AND GREEN

Body.—Grass-green seal's fur, ribbed with gold wire.
Wings.—Feather from the wing or tail of a grouse.
Hackle.—Ginger cock.
Tail.—Golden pheasant tippet.

HALF STONE

Body.—Upper half mole's fur spun on yellow silk; lower half yellow silk or primrose floss.
Hackle.—Honey dun cock, which may be carried half-way down the body.

This is a prime favourite in the West of England, and kills well when nymph fishing. Turing, in his *Trout*

Fishing, suggests that it is probably mistaken for the March Brown nymph, and I think that he is probably correct.

HEN PHEASANT AND YELLOW

Body.—Yellow seal's fur, ribbed with gold wire.
Wings.—Quill feather of hen pheasant's wing.
Hackle.—Hen pheasant, small wing feather.
Tail.—Golden pheasant tippet or scarlet ibis.

A very useful fly for both sea trout and brown trout.

IRON BLUE DUN

Body.—Mole's fur spun on ruddy brown silk.
Wings.—Starling's wing feather dyed blue-black.
Hackle.—Brownish olive cock.
Tail.—Three whisks of hackle.

Dry fly used extensively on South Country streams. The Dark Watchett is a good hackled pattern.

MALLARD AND CLARET

Body.—Deep claret seal's fur, ribbed with gold wire.
Wings.—Mallard's wing feather.
Hackle.—Dyed deep claret.
Tail.—Three fibres of golden pheasant tippet.

This is one of the best flies for sea trout and loch fishing. There are several variations of the dressing.

MARCH BROWN (Wet Pattern)

Body.—Hare's fur, ribbed with yellow silk.
Wings.—Inner feather of a hen pheasant, or from the tail of a partridge.
Hackle.—Feather from the back of a partridge.
Tail.—Two strands of partridge's tail feather.

There is no end to the number of March Brown dressings; every fly-tier seems to have his own particular fancy, but the above is fairly typical of the wet-fly recipes. For dry flies stiff brown speckled cock's hackles are employed.

MAY-FLIES

It is hopeless to attempt to give any dressings of May-flies which might be regarded as generally representative of the thousand and one dressings that pass over the tackle-dealer's counter. I content myself with quoting two or three from accredited authorities.

HALFORD (Dry Fly)

Body.—Raffia grass, ribbed crimson silk.
Wings.—Natural American wood-duck.
Hackle.—Shoulder of medium olive cock's; ribbing hackle of pale ginger cock's.
Tail.—Three strands of bronze Mallard.
Head.—Peacock harl.

WOOLLEY (Wet Fly)

Body.—Yellow lamb's wool, ribbed with gold wire.
Wings.—Speckled grey mallard feather dyed greenish yellow.
Hackle.—Ginger cock dyed yellow.
Tail.—Three strands from cock pheasant's tail feather.

BERNARD's (Spent Gnat—"Shaving-brush")

Body.—White wool, ribbed with doubled black tying silk.
Wings.—Bunches of badger hackle tied back from the eye of the hook.

Hackle.—Natural black cock.

Tail.—Three strands of black horsehair.

See STRADDLE-BUG.

NYMPHS

See chapter on "Nymph Fishing".

OLIVE DUN

Body.—Seal's fur dyed medium olive.

Wings.—Wing feather of a starling.

Hackle.—Cock dyed olive.

Tail.—Three whisks of hackle.

See BLUE DUN.

OLIVE QUILL

Body.—Peacock quill dyed olive.

Wings.—Wing feather of a starling.

Hackle.—Cock dyed olive, light for the Light Olive, darker for the Dark Olive.

Tail.—Three whisks of hackle.

ORANGE PARTRIDGE

Body.—Orange silk, sometimes ribbed sparsely with gold wire or tinsel.

Hackle.—Mottled wing of a partridge.

A famous Yorkshire pattern which will kill all the year round. Imitating in a general sort of way sundry of the *Perlidæ*, it has been a recognised killer on North Country streams from time immemorial, but its merits have won for it distinction far and wide—even on the Hampshire chalk streams. On the Test, Lunn brought out a special gold-ribbed pattern of it which, according to Major J. W. Hills, "is invaluable for both trout and grayling, in all weathers and waters".

ORANGE QUILL

Body.—Stripped condor quill dyed hot orange.
Wings.—Starling's wing feather.
Hackle.—Ginger cock.
Tail.—Three fibres as hackle.

PALE OLIVE

See OLIVES.

PETER ROSS

Body.—Top half red seal's fur, lower half silver tinsel, ribbed with silver oval.
Wings.—Teal.
Hackle.—Black hen.
Tail.—Tippet.

The Peter Ross is what Cotton would have called one of the "Matadores" for sea trout and lake brown trout.

PHEASANT TAIL (Payne Collier's Original Dressing as given in A. Courtney Williams's *Trout Flies*)

Body.—Very dark harl of a cock pheasant's tail feather, with four turns of round gold twist.
Hackle.—Honey dun.
Tail.—Three long red harls from a saddle hackle.

Well-known West Country fly now widely used. Usually fished wet.

POULT BLOA

Body.—Light yellow silk.

Hackle.—A feather from under wing of a young grouse.

Well-known Yorkshire fly useful when the Pale Watery Dun is on or is due to appear.

RED PALMER

Body.—Bronze peacock harl, ribbed with gold wire or tinsel.
Hackle.—Red cock, run from shoulder to tail.

RED QUILL

Body.—Peacock quill dyed dark red.
Wings.—Feather from a starling's wing.
Hackle.—Red cock.
Tail.—Three fibres of hackle.

RED SPINNER

Body.—Crimson floss silk, ribbed with gold wire.
Wings.—Feather from a starling's wing.
Hackle.—Red cock.
Tail.—Three fibres of hackle.

RED UPRIGHT

Body.—Peacock quill dyed dull red.
Hackle.—Red cock.
Tail.—Three fibres of hackle.

A West Country pattern also in use on the South Country streams, fished both wet and dry.

RUSTY BLUE

Body.—Hare's fur, ribbed with gold tinsel.
Hackle.—Rusty blue cock.
Tail.—Three fibres of hackle.

Rusty Red

Body.—Same as Rusty Blue.
Hackle and Tail.—Rusty red cock.

Rusty Variant

Body.—Orange floss silk.
Wings.—Partridge.
Hackle.—Rusty dun cock.

Sand Fly

Body.—Buff fur.
Wings.—Starling.
Hackle.—Ginger cock.

Sedge (Cinnamon)

Body.—Old-gold floss silk.
Wings.—Ruddy brown feather from a brown owl's wing.
Hackle.—Ginger cock, ribbed up the body.

An autumn fly that kills on the South Country streams, fished dry when the Sedges are abroad. Usually fished wet in the North.

Sedge (Red)

Body.—Indian red floss silk, ribbed with gold wire.
Wings.—Brown partridge feather.
Hackle.—Red cock, ribbed up the body.

Silver Doctor

Body.—Silver tinsel, ribbed with silver oval.
Wings.—Mixed strands of red, yellow and green with strips of mallard at the sides.

Hackle.—White cock dyed light blue.
Tail.—Golden pheasant tippet.

A splendid sea trout fly.

SILVER HORNS (Ronalds's Pattern)

Body.—Black ostrich harl tied with black silk and
finished off.
Wings.—Feather from the wing of a cock blackbird.
Hackle.—Small black cock.
Horns.—Grey feather of a mallard.

SNIPE BLOA, *alias* SNIPE AND YELLOW

Body.—Straw-coloured silk.
Hackle.—Feather from inside jack snipe's wing.

Another favourite North Country pattern fished wet.
It has been found useful in nymph fishing on South
Country streams.

STRADDLE-BUG

A strong impression prevails in certain quarters that
the original artificial Straddle-bug was invented by the
late Sir John Ward, and was dressed thus:

Body.—Raffia grass, ribbed with black silk.
Inner Hackle.—Light orange cock.
Outer Hackle.—Bronze mallard.
Tail.—Three strands of pheasant tail.

A variation might be made by substituting ginger
cock for the inner hackle, and the breast feather of a
French partridge for the outer. This for dry-fly work.
For wet fly the inner hackle might be omitted and the
French partridge left long.

"Straddle-bug" is a term which has been very

loosely applied to hackled May-flies. To-day it is probably mostly applied to the French partridge series. It is most popular on the South Country streams and on the Irish loughs—particularly Erne. In appearance it suggests the Spent Gnat, but, rather strangely, it kills well a few days before the May-fly comes on in strength, when it is possibly taken for the nymph.

TEAL AND BLACK

Body.—Black seal's fur, ribbed with silver oval.
Wings.—Teal.
Hackle.—Black cock.
Tail.—Golden pheasant tippet.

TEAL AND GREEN

Body.—Green wool, ribbed with silver oval.
Wings, hackle and *tail* as in Teal and Black.

The last two are good loch flies.

TUP'S INDISPENSABLE (Woolley's Pattern as given in his *Modern Trout Fly Dressing*)

Body.—Creamy pink dubbing, three turns yellow tying silk at tail.
Hackle and *whisks.*—Brassy cock.

Originally a Devon fly, "Tup's" is now well known on most of our rivers.

WATERHEN BLOA

Body.—Yellow silk, waxed and dubbed with mole's fur.
Hackle.—A feather from the underside of a waterhen's wing.

One of the most useful of the North Country

"spider" flies. It will kill all the year round fished wet, and has proved effective in nymph fishing.

WICKHAM'S FANCY

Body.—Flat gold tinsel, ribbed with fine gold wire.
Wings.—Medium starling.
Hackle.—Red cock, run from shoulder to tail.
Tail.—Two strands of the hackle.

One of the most popular of fancy trout—and gray-ling—flies, especially on South Country rivers, where many a fly fisher's creed is, "When all else fails, try a Wickham".

WINTER BROWN

Body.—Orange silk, well waxed, with a turn or two of bronze peacock harl towards the head.
Hackle.—Feather from the inside of a woodcock's wing.

One of the earliest of river flies, known also as the Dark Woodcock.

WOODCOCK AND YELLOW

Body.—Bright yellow silk.
Hackle.—Feather from the inside of a woodcock's wing.

YELLOW DUN (Ronalds's Pattern)

Body.—Yellow mohair, mixed with a little pale blue fur from a mouse. Or yellow silk waxed, and with the least blue rabbit fur spun upon it, and ribbed with yellow silk.
Wings.—Upright, from the lightest part of a young starling's quill feather.
Hackle.—Light yellow dun.

YELLOW BADGER

Body.—Yellow tying silk.
Hackle.—Badger cock.
Tail.—Two or three fibres of hackle.

YELLOW PARTRIDGE

Body.—Bright yellow silk.
Hackle.—Greyish brown feather from back of a partridge.

Another popular pattern in the Yorkshire Partridge series.

CHAPTER XXV

WHAT'S WHAT IN TROUT FISHING

BACKING.—A fine strong line spliced to, and behind, the ordinary dressed reel line. Wound on first, it fills up the spool to a good working level for the reel line proper, and acts as a reserve in cases of emergency when a powerful fish runs off the whole of the dressed line.

BADGER.—Hen's or cock's (usually the latter) neck feather used in fly-dressing, the centre of which is black, or nearly so, with white or cream tipped fibres.

BLOA, BLEA or BLAE.—Literally the colour of a dark threatening sky—leaden or livid. It is a North Country term, and was originally used to denote hackled flies, such as the Waterhen Bloa, Poult Bloa, Snipe Bloa or Blae and Black, which imitate insects having dark grey or bluish-grey wings.

BLOW-LINE.—Either a fine undressed silk line or a length of floss silk, which, instead of being cast in the ordinary way, is allowed to be carried out over the water by the breeze and, humoured by the raising or lowering of the rod point, keeps the fly lightly riding on the surface. Mostly used in May-fly dapping.

BOB FLY.—The top dropper on a wet-fly cast, which is fished so that the bob dances on the surface of the water.

BOBBING.—A North Country synonym for dibbing, bushing or shade fishing, a method of fishing in which a live insect, such as the blue-bottle, is impaled on the hook, and dangled on the surface of the water from the cover afforded by a convenient bush.

BULGING.—A phenomenon common on the chalk streams when the trout are feeding on nymphs or freshwater shrimps, causing a sort of slight upheaval of the surface of the water without actually breaking that surface.

BUSTARD.—A North Country name for the big nocturnal moths, the Ghost Moths and others of the *Hepialidæ*, which flit over the meadows on summer evenings. It is also applied to the artificial moths, rough imitations of the above, which are used in night fishing on the Eden and Border rivers.

BUTT.—The thick end of the rod; often employed to denote the bottom section of the rod terminating in the butt. To "give the trout the butt", or to "show it the butt", is to exert heavy pressure on the fish by pointing the rod backward over the shoulder, so that the butt is towards the fish.

B.W.O.—The Blue-winged Olive Dun.

CAST.—To throw out the line over the water; the act of throwing the line; the particular method by which the line is thrown; the length of gut, or hair, usually about 3 yds. in length, between the end of the reel line and the dry-fly man's fly or the wet-fly man's tail fly; a selection of patterns of fly, tail fly and droppers, used in conjunction in wet-fly fishing.

CHECK.—The pawl-and-ratchet device inside the reel, which places a partial restraint on the free run of the line when a hooked fish makes its rush, and produces the "music of the reel".

COCK.—A dry fly is said to cock when it rides the surface of the water upright and perkily, like the natural insect, instead of floating in, apparent, lifeless helplessness on its side.

CREEL.—A fisherman's basket; to land, and pop in the creel, a fish.

CREEPER.—The larval form of the Stone-fly, best known when it invades the thin edges of the rocky streams previous to crawling out of the water to undergo its metamorphosis into the perfect fly. It is then a favourite bait in the North of England and Scotland, and is greedily taken by the trout.

CRUISER.—A trout which, instead of remaining in one spot and taking the flies which come within its ken, moves hither and thither, indulging in a promenade lunch.

CUSS, *alias* FISHERMAN'S CURSE.—So called on account of the language it is calculated to inspire, this is a tiny specimen of the *Diptera*, or two-winged flies, which hovers over the water—and frequently falls in—at times in myriads, when the trout feed on it gluttonously to the exclusion of all else, the angler's artificials included.

DAMPER.—A case—an oilskin tobacco-pouch makes a good one—containing layers of wet felt, between which gut casting-lines are carried. This ensures their always being ready for use when wanted, avoiding the delay otherwise entailed by having to soak them.

DAPPING.—Usually used to denote blow-line fishing with the May-fly or Daddy-long-legs as practised extensively on the Irish loughs.

DELIVERY.—The forward throw in making a cast.

DIBBING.—See BOBBING.

DOCK GRUB.—A large yellowish-white caterpillar, the larva of the Ghost Moth, found at the roots of the dock, on which it feeds. It is also known as the Docken Grub. Used as a bait, the trout take it eagerly.

DRAG.—The pull of the line which draws the fly out of its course down the current, or which holds it with suggestive unnaturalness against the current, arousing the suspicions of a discerning trout. Drag is the dry-fly fisher's bugbear, and constantly taxes his skill to overcome it.

DRAKE.—The May-fly, of which there are two closely allied species, *Ephemera danica* and *E. vulgata*. The former is the best known and most widely distributed. On first emerging from its husk as the sub-imago it is known as the Green Drake. After shedding a further filmy covering, the female is called the Grey Drake and the male the Black Drake. When the Grey Drake finally, after discharging its eggs, goes west, falls exhausted on the water, it is known as the Spent Gnat.

DRIFTING DOWN.—Casting a fly downstream with a slack line to a feeding fish, allowing the lure to fall above the fish and drift down to it.

DROPPER.—One of a series of flies attached to the gut casting line at intervals of 18 in. or more (according to the number used) above the tail fly or point. They are attached to the main casting line by short lengths of gut of 2½ in. or so.

DRY FLY.—An artificial fly which is fished floating upon the surface of the water, the method of fishing the floating fly.

DUB.—A quiet length or pool of some depth between more rapid portions of the river. Here the current is imperceptible.

DUBBING.—Loose fibres of fur or hair "spun" on to the tying silk in fly-dressing to help to form the body. The silk is first well waxed, after which the dubbing is worked on evenly with the finger and thumb; dressing a fly with dubbing.

DUN.—Any fly of the *Ephemeridæ* in the sub-imago stage, *i.e.* when it first emerges from the husk and appears as a winged insect, previous to its final metamorphosis.

ENTRY.—The curve described by the line at the point of its progress when changing from the back cast to the forward throw. A sharp curve, almost an angle, is known as a narrow entry; a bellying curve as a wide, or broad, entry.

EYED HOOKS.—Hooks, especially those used in dry-fly fishing, the ends of the shanks of which are twisted into an eyelet, so that they can be knotted on the gut instead of being whipped on in the old-fashioned style.

FANCY.—An artificial fly not imitating a natural insect.

FINE, or FINE DOWN.—Said of a river after a flood, when it is clearing in density and abating in volume.

FLIGHT.—An arrangement of hooks on gut designed for a special purpose, notably for spinning a bait.

FLOATER.—A dry fly, which floats upon the surface of the water.

FOLLOW THROUGH.—In casting, the forward motion of the rod after the forward impetus has been given to the line.

FRESH, or FRESHET.—A flood, more or less sudden, caused by heavy rains. In some localities the term suggests something a little less violent than a flood; in fact, something more in the nature of a "brimmer" as compared with a "bumper".

FURNACE.—A fly dresser's term for a hackle, or neck feather, with a black centre and red edges, such as is used in tying the Coch-y-bonddu.

GNAT.—See SPENT GNAT.

GREENHEART.—A tree, native of Guiana, whose timber possesses steel-like properties, rendering it exceptionally suitable for rod-building; often applied to a rod made of this timber.

GROUND-BAIT.—Loose bait thrown into a swim to attract the fish to the spot where the baited hook is then introduced. Ground-baiting is severely deprecated in most trout-fishing circles.

HANG (*Scotice*, "HING").—The tail of a pool, where the water glides smoothly before breaking into the rapid below, a favourite haunt of trout.

HACKLE.—The narrow neck feather of a domestic fowl, tied in at the shoulder of the fly to represent the insect's legs; a feather, or portion of a feather, from any other bird used in a similar manner; to dress a fly with a hackle; a fly dressed with body and hackle, but having no wings.

HEAD-AND-TAIL RISE.—The rise of a fish which breaks the water first with its head, and again with the upper tip of its tail.

HONEY DUN.—Describes a hackle with a grey centre with a suggestion of gold at the edges.

HOOK-BAIT.—The bait on the hook, as distinct from Ground-bait.

HUNG UP.—An angler is said to be hung up when his fly or tackle fouls a tree, snag, or other entanglement.

JACK.—The male Stone-fly, which is easily distinguished by its inferior size compared with that of the female, and the shortness of its wings, which are useless for flight. Cotton made the mistake of supposing the Jack to be an immature Stone-fly in the process of development.

LEADER.—A term common in America, and occasionally used in Britain, to denote the gut casting-line.

LEASH.—In wet-fly fishing it is the general rule to use three flies—a tail fly and two droppers. These three flies are frequently referred to as a leash.

LINK.—A single strand of gut, several of which are knotted together to form the cast.

LOCK-FAST JOINTS.—Rod ferrules fitted with various devices for the prevention of the sections of the rod throwing apart when the cast is made. They are fast falling out of favour owing to the exactness with which the modern plain ferrules fit into one another, so that a throw-out with them is almost unheard of.

MAGGOT.—The larva of the Blue-bottle, or Blow-fly, a bait so attractive to fish that the breeding of it is now an industry in itself.

MAY-FLY.—The Drake, Green, Grey, or Black. Some entomologists classify all the *Ephemeridæ* as May-flies, no matter at what time of the year they appear, which practice is apt to be confusing to the angler. In many parts of the Northern Counties and over the Border where the Stone-fly is abundant and the Green Drake scarce, the former is known as the May-fly.

NEEDLES.—Small, slender *Perlidæ*, members of the Stone-fly family, whose wings fold flat on the back in narrow compass. The imitations are known by such names as Needle Brown, Dark Needle, Spanish Needle, etc.

NYMPH.—An *Ephemerid* in its larval stage at any period between its hatching from the egg and the bursting of its husk whence it emerges as the sub-imago in a winged state. A trout is said to be nymphing when it is feeding upon these larvæ as they swim about under water or as they are in the act of rising to the surface to undergo their transformation to the winged stage.

PALMER.—An artificial fly dressed to imitate a hairy caterpillar, in which the hackle is wound on from shoulder to tail. As the trout can have a very limited acquaintance with the natural "woolly bear", it is doubtful for what they take them—probably simply for something that looks good to eat.

PANNIER.—A fisherman's basket, synonymous with CREEL.

PATERNOSTER.—A form of tackle consisting of a plummet at the end of the line, which anchors it in position, and one or more hooks attached to the line higher up by short links.

PLAY.—Treatment of the trout, by giving and recovering line at discretion after being hooked, in the attempt to bring it to the landing-net; the elasticity of the rod; the whippy rod is said to have more play than the stiff one.

PLUG.—An artificial lure of American origin, fearfully and wonderfully fashioned, which darts, dives or wiggles, but does not spin. Its antics are supposed to represent movements of a wounded or panic-stricken fish.

POINT.—The tail fly on a wet-fly cast: the thin end of the rod top; the thin end of the cast to which, in dry-fly fishing, the fly is tied.

POOL.—See DUB.

POULT.—A young grouse, from under whose wing is taken the feather with which the Poult Bloa is hackled.

PRIEST.—No doubt facetiously so called because it administers the last rites to the captured fish. A form of small bludgeon, often of metal, with which the trout is killed by being struck on the back of the head.

QUILL.—Used extensively in fly-dressing, is usually prepared from one of the fibres of a peacock's tail-feather from which the fluff has been scraped off. It is used dyed or undyed for the bodies of flies. The term is also used to designate a fly which has a quill body, such as the Red Quill or Olive Quill.

RECOVERY.—The lifting and flinging back of the line previous to making the forward cast.

REEL.—The winch or pirn attached to the rod on which the line is wound.

REEL LINE.—The line which, when not extended in fishing, is wound on the reel, as distinct from the casting line of gut. Also it is sometimes used to distinguish it from the backing—which is likewise wound on the reel.

RISE.—The upward movement of the trout for the purpose of taking a fly from the surface or under the surface; the appearance of a number of natural flies on the water at or about the same time.

SCALE READING.—Ascertaining much of the life-history of a fish from the examination, under a magnifying glass, of the rings on each of its scales. This reveals, among other minor things, the age of the trout, at what age it first spawned, and how many times it has spawned since.

SCARAB.—An invention of A. Holden Illingworth, consisting of a transparent sheath in which the natural minnow is encased when spinning. By its use the same minnow will serve quite a long time, instead of being mauled by the first trout that takes it.

SCOUR.—A portion of the river running quickly over a gravel bed; to clean and toughen worms by allowing them to thread their way through damp moss lightly pressed together.

SHOOTING THE LINE.—Holding a loop of the line in reserve in the left hand while making a cast until the forward throw is almost complete, when the extra line is released and shoots forward through the rings.

SNECK BEND.—Describes a hook the point and barb of which, instead of being in the same plane as the shank, are turned to one side.

SPEAR.—A short blunt spike which may be fixed in the butt of the rod, so that, when not in action, and the spear is thrust into the ground, the rod stands upright and the danger of its being trodden on is avoided.

SPENT GNAT.—The Grey Drake, or female May-fly, after it has discharged its eggs and falls with outstretched wings on the water, its mission in life fulfilled.

SPIDER.—A lightly dressed hackle fly of the type known as "Yorkshire flies".

SPINNER.—One of the *Ephemeridæ* which has reached the imago stage; a piece of tackle designed to make a minnow spin when drawn through the water; a lure which spins when drawn through the water, such as the Halcyon Spinner.

SPLIT-CANE.—A rod, hexagonal in section, which is composed of six strips of bamboo, planed to fit each other and glued together into a solid whole.

STICKLE.—A shallow, rippling, rapid run of water over a gravel bed.

STREAM.—A portion of the river which is very perceptibly flowing, as distinct from a DUB or POOL; a river, a brook, or burn.

STRIKE.—To tighten the line on a fish which has just mouthed the fly or bait in order to drive in the hook over the barb.

SUCTION FERRULES.—Plain ferrules so carefully fitted to one another that they will not throw out in casting.

TAIL FLY.—The end fly on the cast when fishing the wet fly.

TAILING.—Said of trout when they are feeding head downwards on the bottom, or perhaps on a weed-bed, with their tails almost perpendicular above them.

THREAD-LINE FISHING.—Angling with a light fixed-spool reel, in connection with which is used a fine line no thicker than sewing cotton.

TOP.—The uppermost joint of a rod.

TROLL.—To spin a minnow by trailing it from a

moving boat, in the manner in which big trout are caught on the Irish loughs.

VARIANT.—A style of dry fly invented by the late Dr William Baigent, of Northallerton. It is a long-hackled sparsely dressed fly, tied in many patterns which have proved deadly on many trout streams both in the North and South.

WADING STOCKINGS.—Mackintosh protective coverings for the legs which reach well up on the thigh.

WADING TROUSERS.—Might be described as wading stockings which join at the fork and are continued in a body-piece to the armpits.

WANING.—Said of a river in which the flood water is falling.

WAXING.—Said of a river when the flood water is rising; rubbing tying silk with cobbler's wax or some substitute possessing similar properties.

WEEDS.—Vegetable growths in a river, most common in a sluggish water.

WET FLY.—An artificial fly which is fished under water.

WHISKS.—Hair-like appendages protruding from the posterior of a fly.

WHIP.—To bind with silk or thread.

YORKSHIRE FLIES.—Sparsely hackled wingless flies popular among anglers on the Yorkshire and other North Country moorland trout streams.

APPENDIX

EVOLUTION OF THE FIXED-SPOOL REEL

ONE of the most discussed trout-fishing topics of modern angling times is the fixed-spool reel, which is practically synonymous with thread-line fishing. I have found that there is a good deal of misconception abroad as to origin of this method of light bait casting, and, having been in close touch with the inventor during its development, I probably know as much as, if not more than, any other man living about the movement. That being so, I feel constrained to place on record here a brief summary of the historical facts.

From time immemorial the angler, in casting his spinning flight, had done so from his line coiled upon the ground, in the boat, or elsewhere, until, in the latter part of the nine-teenth century, P. D. Malloch mechanised the system, and the first patent for the "Malloch Casting Reel" was taken out in 1884. The Malloch is a combination of the principles of the fixed-spool and the revolving drum. During the casting the spool is stationary, its axis parallel with the rod, and the line is drawn off the end of the spool in straightening coils; the spool is then turned so that it is brought into a vertical position for acting as a revolving drum, operated by the handle in the ordinary way.

The Malloch was designed for fishing a comparatively heavy line and bait in salmon and pike angling, and, with the cast putting one turn into the line for each coil thrown off, kinking trouble quickly arose, to counteract which the drum was made reversible. Various improvements have been added at other times, and the Malloch is to-day the favourite spinning reel among the heavy-weights of many salmon and pike fishers.

It was not, however, until the first decade of the present century that the fixed-spool reel for light bait casting made its appearance in the shape—and it was a curious shape—of the "Illingworth No. 1". The inventor, Alfred Holden Illingworth, a member of a family long and honourably connected with the Bradford worsted trade, set himself the task of producing a reel which would cast the lightest of minnows on the finest of tackle, avoid danger of breakage by the operation of an adjustable friction clutch, avoid over-run, take out in the recovery the kink put into the line in the casting, spin with a multiplying gear a minnow down the edges of shallow streams, and do it all with the minimum of exertion and a light wand of the fly rod type. He did it.

The "Illingworth No. 1" was patented in 1905, and first came into prominent notice in 1908 at the International Tournament, when, in the 3 drs. light bait event, Illingworth, with an aggregate of three casts, threw 309 ft. against the runner-up's 258 ft., and the third man's 220 ft.

The "Illingworth No. 1" was a complete breakaway from reel tradition. Hitherto inventors had started with something approximately resembling an orthodox reel, and had worked on that foundation. Illingworth did not; apparently he started with a worsted spinning spindle and harnessed that and sundry of its kindred associations to his purpose. The result was a weird contraption, the frame of which was a circular plate of aluminium fixed to the bracket for attachment to the rod. Sunk in one side of this plate a metal disc was revolved by a handle and operated the working parts on the other side. The spool, in this case a solid wooden cylinder with a conical nose and a general resemblance to the spool in a weaver's shuttle, stood out above the frame and disc, and on the level part of the spool was wound the line by a "flier" that whizzed round the spool, and so took out all the twists the cast had put in. As the flier wound on the line, the spool was mechanically moved up and down, so that the coils were laid on in open spirals, giving what has been lately known as the "cross-wind" effect. The old reel has long since been superseded, but in one respect its casting power has never been surpassed, for there was no flange for the line to friction against as it was drawn off. The spool never revolved except when the pull of a fish overcame the resistance of the friction brake and drew off line until the reel resumed control. The flier was geared to such a speed that the minnow, cast upstream into thin water, could be brought down the stream just sufficiently faster than the current to cause it to spin attractively.

No sooner were the capabilities—or alleged capabilities—of the Illingworth invention noised abroad than certain sections of the angling public howled hysterically. If such a diabolical poaching engine were let loose on our streams, leaving wholesale destruction in its wake, trout fishing was doomed to speedy extinction! From the diatribes of some of the frenzied alarmists which appeared in the Angling Press one might have gathered that the "Illingworth Reel" was the recognised synonym for "Wholesale Massacre", "Unrestrained Blood Lust", "Slaughter of the Innocents", etc. Happily, in spite of these diatribes, nobody seemed one penny the worse, and although the tackle market is now flooded with fixed-spool reels embodying the fundamental features of the "Illingworth No. 1", our trout streams are far from depleted.

The special purpose for which the Illingworth was designed was to catch trout with the spinning minnow in low clear water that by the majority of anglers would be regarded as hopeless. In reasonably skilful hands it would often do so; at other times it would not, just as the fixed-spool reels of to-day occasionally fail us, spin they the lure never so seductively.

In writing about these early forms of the fixed-spool reel, there is one pattern which certainly deserves passing notice, albeit, so far as my knowledge goes, it only made one public appearance. Nor can I fix the date of that appearance, which was made at a French casting tournament in the early part of the century, though whether before or after the appearance of the Illingworth I do not remember. It was a crude affair, consisting of a round tin—cocoa or mustard, I wot not—rigged on the butt so that the cylinder lay parallel with the rod. A thread-like line was wound on the tin, and cast off the end of it as from the spool of the "Illingworth No. 1". With this rude apparatus the competitor made some astonishing casts, but how he got the line back on the mustard tin I have completely forgotten.

The first serious rival to challenge the "Illingworth No. 1" was the "Holroyd-Smith Reel", patented in 1907. This was a good reel, embodying some capital features, but, so far as I could gather, the inventor had unintentionally infringed the Illingworth patents, and so the reel was not offered for sale.

The first fixed-spool reel to be put on the market after the first Illingworth was the "Chippindale", patented in 1909. Writers who have touched, generally very sketchily, on the development of the fixed-spool reel for light bait casting, have usually ignored the "Chippindale" or merely mentioned it by name. As a matter of fact it marked a stage in the evolution of the new type of reel by introducing a new shape of spool that, with modifications, was widely adopted by later inventors. Otherwise the "Chippindale" made no advance. It was worked on the principle of the "Malloch", but with the difference that the spool retained its horizontal position throughout cast and recovery. There was no friction clutch, no multiplying gear, no flier to take out the kink.

Perhaps the greatest good the "Chippindale" did was to spur on Illingworth to bring out his No. 2 pattern. This is not founded on hearsay; Illingworth discussed the matter freely with me himself. I was with him on the morning when the first "No. 2" (in the rough) reached him from the maker, and we tried it out together on the grass. For one thing Illingworth wanted to get down the price, which was for the "No. 1" £2 : 17 : 6, while the "Chippindale" was offered "complete with three spools of different sizes, 15s.". Also he wanted more accommodation for the line than the cylindrical spool afforded (which was 40 yds.), and he wanted a firmer wind. These he obtained by the adoption of a spool somewhat similar in outline to that of the "Chippindale", and the "Illingworth No. 2" was patented in 1910.

This reel possessed, in effect, all the special features of the "No. 1" in a more compact form plus sundry improvements, and may be regarded in a general way as the prototype of every light fixed-spool reel that has since appeared. The "Chippindale", with its limited merits, did not attain a wide popularity, and the "Illingworth No. 2", which was sold at £1 : 12 : 6, geared 2 to 1, or £1 : 15s., geared 3 to 1, practically held undisputed sway until the "Illingworth No. 3" made its debut in 1913. In general appearance this model closely resembled the "No. 2", but included a few further improvements, and it is to-day a common object of the riverside and a familiar feature in tackle-dealers' catalogues.

Almost simultaneously with the appearance of the "Illingworth No. 3", the "Carswell" reel saw the light of publicity, and was promptly challenged as an infringement of the Illingworth patents. A lengthy correspondence ensued. Counsels' opinions differed as widely as the interests of the two parties seeking them, and, recognising that litigation would be costly to both sides, a compromise was agreed upon, the Carswell Co. being allowed to market their reel at 35s., clearly engraved as a "Modified Illingworth-Carswell" production under licence from the Illingworth people, and on payment of a royalty to them. This royalty was paid from 1914 to 1925, when payment ceased. Inquiries elicited the facts that the Carswell patent had lapsed through neglect to pay the renewal fees. Subsequently the "Modified Illingworth-Carswell" reappeared on the scene as the "Spinet", and has enjoyed a considerable amount of favour—especially in Scotland.

By this time the earlier Illingworth patents, which covered the essential features of the really effective modern light casting reel, had also run out, and this opened the field to the production of several recent variations of the fixed-spool type too well known to need description here.

It is due to the memory of Alfred Holden Illingworth, the father of light-bait casting from the fixed-spool reel, to add that he expended time, money and ingenuity on his invention without one thought of pecuniary gain. It was his hobby, and he deliberately refused to make any personal profit out of it.

The prices quoted in the foregoing are figures which obtained before the post-War advance in cost. A considerable range of these reels is now available at prices varying from roughly £1 : 10s. to about £12 : 12s.

INDEX

237

THE END

Printed in Great Britain by R. & R. CLARK, LIMITED, *Edinburgh*